OUR WAY

4

PREMIUM EDITION

AMOS
PRESCHER
PASQUALIN

Richmond

Richmond

Diretoria: *Paul Berry*
Gerência editorial: *Sandra Possas*
Coordenação de arte: *Christiane Borin*
Coordenação de *bureau*: *Américo Jesus*
Coordenação de revisão: *Katia Gouveia Vitale*
Gerência de produção gráfica: *André Monteiro*
Coordenação de produção gráfica: *Maria de Lourdes Rodrigues*
Gerência de produção industrial: *Wilson Aparecido Troque*

Coordenação do projeto: *Adriana Beatriz Saporito, Ana Lucia Militello, Henrique Zanardi*

Edição de texto: *Adriana Beatriz Saporito, Henrique Zanardi*
Assistência editorial: *Bruna Marini, Camila Carmo da Silva, Kelly Taniguchi, Mariana Zanini, Nathália Horvath*
Preparação de texto: *Maria Estela de Alcântara, Thelma Guimarães*
Revisão linguística: *Raymond Shoulder*
Revisão: *Alexandre Gomes Camarú, Amanda de Lima Lassak, Mariana Mininel de Almeida, Rafael Gustavo Spigel, Roberta Moratto Risther, Vivian Marques Viccino, Viviane Mendes*
Projeto gráfico e edição de arte: *David Urbinatti Netto*
Ilustrações: *Airon Barreto, Eduardo Medeiros*
Criações: *Amanda Savoini, Gisele A. Rocha, Hulda Melo, Talita Guedes, Tangente Design*
Capa: *Amanda Savoini*
Pesquisa iconográfica: *Carol Böck, Marcia Sato, Mariana Veloso Lima*
Tratamento de imagens: *Arleth Rodrigues, Fabio N. Precendo, Pix Art, Wagner Lima*
Diagramação: *Tangente Design*
Pré-impressão: *Alexandre Petreca, Everton L. de Oliveira Silva, Hélio P. de Souza Filho, Marcio H. Kamoto*

Welcome Unit: Luciana Pimentel
Extra Reading: Luciana Silva
Grammar Reference: Carla Maurício Coelho da Silva Vianna
Manual do professor: Luciana Silva, Nelson Mitrano Neto

Dados Internacionais de Catalogação na Publicação (CIP)
(Câmara Brasileira do Livro, SP, Brasil)

Amos, Eduardo
Our way / Eduardo Amos, Elisabeth Prescher, Ernesto Pasqualin. – 7. ed. – São Paulo : Moderna, 2012.

Obra em 4 v. para alunos do 6º ao 9º ano do ensino fundamental.

1. Inglês (Ensino fundamental) 2. Inglês (Ensino fundamental) – Atividades, exercícios etc. I. Prescher, Elisabeth. II. Pasqualin, Ernesto. III. Título.

12-05155 CDD-372.652

Índices para catálogo sistemático:
1. Inglês : Ensino fundamental 372.652

ISBN 978-85-16-07947-5 (LA)
ISBN 978-85-16-07948-2 (LP)

Richmond Publishing
Editora Moderna Ltda.
Rua Padre Adelino, 758 – Belenzinho
São Paulo – SP – Brasil – CEP 03303-904
Central de atendimento ao usuário: 0800 771 8181
www.richmond.com.br
2013

Impresso na China

Créditos das fotos:
Capa: © Barauskaite/Shutterstock
P. 8: © Thinkstock/Getty Images; P. 12: © Mark Schwettmann/Shutterstock; © Luiz C. Ribeiro/Shutterstock; © Mechika/Alamy/Other Images; © LC Moreira/Futura Press; © Thinkstock/Getty Images; © Daniel Wiedemann/Shutterstock; © Giancarlo Liguori/Shutterstock; © Alvaro Pantoja/Shutterstock; P. 13: © Maurício de Sousa Produções; P. 14: © Andrea Danti/Shutterstock; © Patrick Breig/Shutterstock; © Jiri Miklo/Shutterstock; P. 16: © Gorilla/Shutterstock; © Thinkstock/Getty Images; © Upthebanner/Shutterstock; © Fotokostic/Shutterstock; P. 18: Paule Saviano/Alamy/Other Images; © Steve Snowden/Shutterstock; P. 20: © Thinkstock/Getty Images; © Mika Heittola/Shutterstock; © Shutterstock; © DK.samco/Shutterstock; © Thinkstock/Getty Images; © Olinchuk/Shutterstock; © Steamroller Blues/Shutterstock; © AMA/Shutterstock; P. 27: © Sam DCruz/Shutterstock; P. 30: © Thinkstock/Getty Images; © Pojoslaw/Shutterstock; © Karam Miri/Shutterstock; © Petro Feketa/Shutterstock; © Dean Bertoncej/Shutterstock; P. 33: © Camilo Torres/Shutterstock; © Thinkstock/Getty Images; © Simon Bratt/Shutterstock; © Thinkstock/Getty Images; P. 36: © Tristan Tan/Shutterstock; © Luiz Rocha/Shutterstock; © TsR/Shutterstock; © Ingrid Prats/Shutterstock; P. 38: © Randy Miramontez/Shutterstock; P. 41: © Thinkstock/Getty Images; © Thinkstock/Getty Images; © Auremar/Shutterstock; © Sima/Shutterstock; © Thinkstock/Getty Images; © Galina Barskaya/Shutterstock; © Micro10x/Shutterstock; © Thinkstock/Getty Images; © Beto Celli; P. 42: © Sarun T/Shutterstock; © Pi-Lens/Shutterstock; © Thinkstock/Getty Images; P. 44: © Vilena makarica/Shutterstock; P. 47: © Thinkstock/Getty Images; © Kostudio/Shutterstock; P. 48: © Marcelo Liso/Agência Estado; P. 57: © Kuttig Travel /Alamy/Other Images; © Barry King/WireImage/Getty Images; P. 58: © Reprodução; © Reprodução; © Touchstone Pictures/Everett Collection/Grupo Keystone; P. 62: © Featureflash/Shutterstock; © S_bukley/Shutterstock; P. 63: © Blend Images/Shutterstock; © Nicole Gordine/Shutterstock; © Thinkstock/Getty Images; © Patryk Kosmider/Shutterstock; © Thinkstock/Getty Images; © Juriah Mosin/Shutterstock; P. 64: © Reprodução; P. [illegible]: © Reprodução; © Reprodução; P. 68: © Thinkstock/Getty Images; P. 70: © Radius Images/Glow Images; © Hannamariah/Shutterstock; © Hamurishi/Shutterstock; © Andresr/Shutterstock; © Thinkstock/Getty Images; © Monkey Business Images/Shutterstock; © T[illegible] Freeze/Shutterstock; © Monkey Business Images/Shutterstock; P. 84: © João Candido Portinari/Projeto Portinari; © João Candido Portinari/Projeto Portinari; P. 87: © Thinkstock/Getty Images; © Pascal Deloche/Godong/Corbis/Latinstock; © Phase4Photography/Shutterstock; P. 90: © Tarsila do Amaral Empreendimentos – Acervo Artístico-Cultural dos Palácios do Governo do Estado de São Paulodigo; P. 92: © Dorivan Marinho/Folhapress; © Saul Loeb/AFP Photo/Getty Images; © Fabrice Coffrini/AFP/Getty Images; P. 94: © Masterfile/Other Images; © Fernando Favoretto/Criar Imagem; P. 95: © John Warburton-Lee Photography/Leelu Morris/Diomedia; P. 108: © Brian A Jackson/Shutterstock; © Nadezhda Kulagina/Shutterstock; © Stephen Coburn/Shutterstock; © Has[illegible] Group Production Studio/Shutterstock; © Ambrozinio/Shutterstock; © PavelSvoboda/Shutterstock; p. 110: © Thinkstock/Getty Images; P. 116: © Thinkstock/Getty Images; © Eric Isselée/Shutterstock.

Contents

Welcome Unit

Simple Actions that Change the World

Really? How?
We're organizing a cleanup event in the neighborhood and the recycling of the garbage.
Hi, Miranda! What are you looking at?
These are the photos of the Volunteer Day we took part in last year.
PHOTO
What were your sisters doing here?
They were reading books to blind people.
And what were you doing here?
I was taking care of abandoned animals.
That's cool! Congratulations!
Thank you! I'm always ready to work as a volunteer.

1 Write sentences that describe each picture. Take these sentences from the text.

1

My friends and I are going to spend one day at a retirement home, playing games with elderly people.

2

____
____
____

3

____
____
____

4

____
____
____

2 Match these words to their definitions.

1 volunteer
2 retirement
3 abandoned
4 elderly
5 recycling

a [ ] The act of retiring (to stop working, usually because of the age).
b [ ] Being old or near old age.
c [ ] The act of treating or processing used or waste material so as to make it suitable for reuse.
d [ ] Discarded, rejected.
e [*1*] A person who voluntarily offers his or her services.

3 Write the correct letter in the correct place and find the message.

23 18 15 20 5	The Simple Past of "write" is ______.
2 (B) **5** 7 1 (A) 14	The show ______ an hour ago.
12 5 6 (F) 20	The kids ______ home after lunch.
3 1 13 5	They ______ back before dinner.
2 **15** 21 (U) 7 8 20 (T)	Mom ______ a new computer.
13 1 4 5	Grandma ______ a chocolate cake.
13 **5** 20	I ______ my classmates at school yesterday.
1 **20** 5	The dog ______ its food.
20 **15** 15 11	We ______ many pictures at the zoo.
2 18 15 21 7 8 20	The Simple Past of "bring" is ______.
4 18 **15** 22 5	He ______ his car to the garage.
6 (F) **15** 21 14 4 (D)	I ______ my book under the sofa.
11 14 5 23	We ______ the correct answer.
6 12 5 23	The Simple Past of "fly" is ______.
2 18 **15** 11 5	He ______ his leg and is in hospital.
20 1 (A) **21** 7 8 (H) 20	She ______ me English last year.
18 5 1 4 (D)	I ______ a good book last week.

1 What Will Life Be Like?

1 Look at the following text and picture and answer.

1 What kind of text is it?

2 What is the text about?

2 Read the following text.

Address: http://articles.famouswhy.com

Find

PEOPLE | REGIONS | ASK | WEB | FORUM | SUBMIT

Born Today | Born Where | Movies | Zodiac | Sites/Blogs

What Will Life Be Like in 2050?

by Cristina Nuta

What picture do you have of the future? Will life be better, worse or the same as now? Futurologists predict that life will probably be very different in 2050 in all fields of activity. TV channels will disappear. Instead, we will choose a programme from a menu and a computer will send the programme directly to our TV set. The same will happen with songs, films, newspapers and books. They will all come to us by computer.

Virtual reality games are already popular. But, by 2050, we will be able to smell and touch the things that we see on television.

Water will be one of our most serious problems. Some futurologists predict that water could be the cause of wars if we don't act now. Demand will increase and there could be serious shortages.

Cars will run very fast on new, clean fuels. Computers will control their speed to prevent accidents and drive them to their destination. Space planes will take people from Los Angeles to Tokyo in just two hours.

Robots will be everywhere: schools, offices, hospitals, shops and homes, and they will replace people in factories.

Medical technology will help blind people to see and deaf people to hear. Scientists will be able to clone people and decide on their appearance, behavior and intelligence – but should they?

Adapted from: <http://articles.famouswhy.com>. Accessed on: April 10, 2012.

3 Go to the glossary at the end of the book. Look up the meaning of these words from the text.

1 shortage ____________________
2 predict ____________________
3 prevent ____________________
4 be able to ____________________

4 Check Yes or No according to your opinion.

1 Is it possible to predict the future? ☐ Yes ☐ No
2 Will it be possible to smell things on a TV screen? ☐ Yes ☐ No
3 Will there be water shortage in the future? ☐ Yes ☐ No
4 Will water be the cause of wars? ☐ Yes ☐ No
5 Will energy be clean? ☐ Yes ☐ No
6 Will robots be everywhere? ☐ Yes ☐ No
7 Will scientists be able to clone people? ☐ Yes ☐ No

5 Read people's opinions about the article on page 8. Then express your opinion.

Address: http://articles.famouswhy.com

Find

Myself 4/2011
No one knows what will happen in 2050, not even scientists.

That Rabia Kid 3/2011
I think this stuff will happen sooner than 2050.

Stephane 12/2010
I think future will be the Anarchy!

Robots Will Take over 11/2010
Robots will take over the world.

Extracted from: <http://articles.famouswhy.com>. Accessed on: May 10, 2012.

Name ____________________ Month/year ____________
____
____

Let's Talk about It

De acordo com o texto, especialistas no estudo do futuro preveem que, em 2050, a vida será muito diferente em todas as atividades. Você concorda? Discorda? Por quê?

6 Look at the pictures. Then practice the predictions with a classmate.

1

Annie / doctor

2

Bob / pilot

3

Cindy and Paul / musicians

A: *What will Annie be?*

B: *I think she will be a doctor.*

4

Larry / singer

5

Kevin and John / painters

6

Daniel / plumber

7

Michelle / computer programmer

8

Kate / sales clerk

7 Write predictions about some people in exercise 6. Use the cues given.

1 Annie *will be a doctor.*

2 Larry ______________________________.

3 Kevin and John ______________________________.

4 Michelle ______________________________.

GRAMMAR

Simple Future

Affirmative: I **will** be a dentist.
'll

Interrogative: **Will** you be a dentist?

Negative: I **will not** be a dentist.
won't

Short answers: Yes, I will.
No, I won't.

Question Words

What will she do tomorrow?
When will he come back?
Where will he spend the weekend?
How will she go there?

O *Simple Future* é usado para expressar decisões tomadas para o futuro e para fazer previsões ou promessas no momento em que se fala.

8 Match the sentences.

1 Grandpa is going to visit us next week.
2 It's going to rain tonight.
3 It's Jane's birthday tomorrow.
4 It's the World Cup final next Saturday.
5 The phone's ringing.

a ( ) I'll watch the game on TV.
b ( ) I'll answer it.
c ( ) I'll bake a cake for him.
d ( ) I'll take the umbrella then.
e ( ) I'll buy her flowers.

9 Answer the questions with the cues given.

1 Where will you go on vacation next year? (beach)

____

2 He won the lottery. What will he do now? (buy a new house)

____

3 Her car is broken. How will she get to the theater? (by taxi)

____

4 When will you phone me? (tonight)

____

10 Look at the pictures and talk to a classmate.

A: *Where did you go last vacation?*
B: *I went to Bahia.*

A: *How about next year?*
B: *Hmm... I think I'll go to Curitiba.*

Rio de Janeiro

Salvador

São Paulo

Fortaleza

Brasília

Florianópolis

Curitiba

Manaus

3 **11** Listen to the story and check.

PLANS / PERSON	JESSICA	MARK	LAURIE	STEVE
buy a house				
buy a yacht				
buy clothes				
do nothing				
go on a cruise				
go to the beach				
open an account				
travel with friends				

GRAMMAR

Verb Tenses

O *Present Continuous* expressa ação em andamento no momento presente:
We **are studying** now.

O *Past Continuous* expressa ação em andamento em determinado momento do passado:
I **was reading** your message yesterday morning.

Going to expressa ação planejada ou decisão tomada:
He **is going to travel** next week.

O *Simple Present* expressa uma ação habitual ou um fato:
He **watches** TV every morning.

O *Simple Past* expressa uma ação passada já concluída:
I **cleaned** my room yesterday.

O *Simple Future* expressa previsões e decisões tomadas no momento da fala:
We **will travel** abroad next year.

12 Answer the questions about yourself.

1 What are you doing now?

____

2 What were you doing an hour ago?

____

3 Where did you go yesterday?

____

4 Who are you going to meet after school today?

____

5 Where do you usually spend your vacation?

____

6 Where will you go next vacation?

____

13 Based on the questions below, write a composition about your life in 2050.

1. How old will you be in 2050?
2. Where will you live: in the country, in the city, on the beach, in the mountains, on a farm, or by a lake?
3. Will you live in a house or in an apartment?
4. What will your profession be?
5. Will you be successful?
6. Will you be married?
7. Will you have children?
8. Will you have possessions? What?
9. Will you help other people?

In 2050, I will be…

FUN

14 Guess their future professions. Then find the words in the wordsearch.

1 She likes to paint. She'll be a ______.

2 She likes to play musical instruments. She'll be a ______.

3 He likes computer programs. He'll be a ______.

4 He likes libraries. He'll be a ______.

5 She likes to build doll houses. She'll be an ______.

6 She likes to study the human body. She'll be a ______.

7 He likes to dance. He'll be a ______.

8 He likes airplanes. He'll be a ______.

9 He likes to fix pipes. He'll be a ______.

10 He likes to repair cars. He'll be a ______.

11 She likes to help sick people. She'll be a ______.

D	A	N	C	E	R	P	E	D	H	S
I	Y	W	K	O	M	N	I	B	C	X
G	A	O	T	R	G	Y	F	L	E	O
L	M	C	L	I	N	T	T	Z	O	X
T	O	B	N	M	U	L	R	N	Z	T
D	N	E	I	C	R	M	E	W	G	E
K	E	P	H	J	S	U	B	D	Q	T
R	P	L	C	B	E	S	M	R	P	V
A	E	V	I	K	B	I	U	O	I	M
D	O	T	A	B	N	C	L	X	W	T
C	M	R	N	Y	R	I	P	T	X	L
S	L	E	C	I	N	A	H	C	E	M
S	T	A	P	I	A	N	R	W	C	B
V	Q	D	E	H	F	P	R	I	X	E
N	C	C	P	O	G	W	S	G	A	S
P	R	O	G	R	A	M	M	E	R	N

4 **Key Language**

act
choose
dancer
decide
dentist
doctor
drive
engineer
hear
help
increase
librarian
mechanic
musician
nurse
painter
pilot
plumber
predict
prevent
programmer
run
see
send
singer
smell
take
touch

Way to Go

1 Answer the questions according to the pictures and make predictions.

1

A: Will she be a teacher in the future?

B: Yes, ______________________________

______________________________.

2

A: What will you wear to go to the movies?

B: ______________________________

to go to the movies.

3

A: Where will they go on their next vacation?

B: ______________________________

New York on their next vacation.

4

A: Will Bob play tennis this weekend?

B: No, ______________________________

______________________________.

2 Complete the sentences. Use the correct tense of the verbs in parentheses.

1 ______________ you ______________ (take) a shower when I called you last night?

2 My little brother ______________ (watch) TV every morning.

3 We ______________ (visit) our cousins in the U.S. next vacation.

4 What ______________ you ______________ (do) at the moment?

5 Where ______________ they ______________ (travel) to on their last vacation?

3 Go back to page 13. Ask the questions from exercise 12 to a classmate. Then write his / her answers below.

1 ______________________________

2 ______________________________

3 ______________________________

4 ______________________________

5 ______________________________

6 ______________________________

4 Read the article below. Circle the verbs in the Simple Future.

Address: http://news.bbc.co.uk

Find

NEWS

News Sport Weather Travel Future TV Radio More

What Will You Be When You Grow up?

By Amber Vially
The New Castle Education Reporter

Frequently adults ask children about their future profession and bring up the question *"What Will You Be When You Grow up?"*
Last week, the traditional question above was asked to children in some primary schools.
Claire,10, is pretty sure that she wants to be a hotel administrator.
"I love to organize things and events. Besides that, I like to deal with people, too. I have a good chance at becoming a hotel administrator but I know I will have to study Math very hard and my mother has helped me a lot with this issue."
And 11-year-old Samira wants to be a TV news anchor. But does she know what a TV news anchor has to do?
"Well, I'm really good at English, very determined, not shy and I want to be famous," she answers.
Keith Carter, 11, was inspired by his neighbor who is a firefighter.
"Mr. Sinclair, my neighbor, is a firefighter in Gleen City and I liked the sound of it. He drives fast red trucks, he also wears helmets and an impressive uniform." And he seems to have a real understanding that firefighters do not just drive around in very fast and big trucks. "They also help people in real trouble. They are very important to the community."
And for the 10-year-old Rosalyn, it's clear that she will become a pharmacist. She is also clear that she will have to study hard, get good grades in order to be able to go to the university. "I want to help people, work in a big pharmaceutical industry as my father does and get lots of money." she added.

Based on: <http://news.bbc.co.uk>. Accessed on: April 10, 2012.

5 Match children and their future profession, according to the text.

1 Claire
2 Samira
3 Keith
4 Rosalyn

a ☐ TV news anchor
b ☐ firefighter
c ☐ hotel administrator
d ☐ pharmacist

6 Based on the text, complete the sentences.

1 According to Claire, a hotel administrator loves ______________________________
____.

2 For a person to be a TV news anchor, he or she has to be ______________________
______________________. That's what ______________________ says.

3 ______________________________ inspired Keith to be a firefighter.

4 Rosalyn wants to be a pharmacist because ______________________________
______________________________ as her father does.

2 Sadako and the Thousand Paper Cranes

1 Answer.

1 When did World War II start? In 1914 or in 1939?

2 What happened in Hiroshima and in Nagasaki in 1945?

2 Read the text about Sadako and the Children's Peace Monument.

On August 6, 1945, the United States Air Force dropped an atomic bomb on Hiroshima, Japan. Sadako Sasaki was living there. She was two years old.

Sadako survived and became a lively and active girl. She enjoyed sports, especially running. In 1954, Sadako won every race at her school and became very popular. In December, she felt the first symptoms of a deadly disease: she felt dizziness and a slight pain under her ears. She had leukemia caused by nuclear radiation.

On February 18, 1955, Sadako was hospitalized. Her courage and determination impressed her classmates.

One day in August her best friend Chizuko visited her. "I know how you can get well," said Chizuko. "Remember the old story about the paper cranes?" she asked.

"Yes, if a sick person folds one thousand paper cranes the gods make her healthy again," replied Sadako.

Then Chizuko took a square piece of paper and folded it over and over.

Chizuko put a paper crane in Sadako's hand and said, "Here is your first one."

Sadako folded many paper cranes. But on October 25 she folded her last crane.

Her classmates had to fold 353 cranes to complete Sadako's one thousand cranes.

Sadako's classmates raised funds to build the Children's Peace Monument in the Peace Memorial Park as a tribute to the children killed by the atomic bomb in Hiroshima.

Based on: <www.hiroshima-is.ac.jp>. Accessed on: May 14, 2012.

3 Write T (true) or F (false), according to the text.

1 ☐ Sadako lived in Hiroshima.
2 ☐ Chizuko and Sadako were friends.
3 ☐ Sadako was born in 1945.
4 ☐ When Sadako was a child she was not healthy.
5 ☐ Sadako liked to run.

4 Answer the questions.

1 How old was Sadako when she discovered that she had leukemia?

____

2 What did Chizuko give her one day in August?

____

3 How many paper cranes did Sadako fold?

____

5 Check the synonyms for the underlined words or phrases of the text.

1 She <u>enjoyed</u> sports, especially running.

a ☐ hated
b ☐ liked
c ☐ didn't like

2 She felt dizziness and a <u>slight</u> pain under her ears.

a ☐ soft
b ☐ strong
c ☐ intense

3 Chizuko took a square piece of paper and folded it <u>over and over</u>.

a ☐ many times
b ☐ only on one side
c ☐ on a table

Let's Talk about It

Hoje em dia, muitos alunos fazem tsurus em dobradura e os enviam ao monumento em memória de Sadako. Na sua opinião, isso é algo importante a ser feito?

6 Look at the pictures and practice the dialogues with a classmate.

1

tablet / Celina

A: *Whose tablet is it?*
B: *It's Celina's.*

2

cell phoes / the boys

A: *Whose cell phones are they?*
B: *They're the boys'.*

3

car / Michael

4

shoes / Mom

5

rackets / my brothers

6

ball / Jane

7

bicycles / your friends

8

skateboard / Bob

7 Write about some items in exercise 6.

1 tablet
That's Celina's tablet.

2 cell phones
Those are the boys' cell phones.

3 skateboard
____

4 shoes
____

5 rackets
____

GRAMMAR

Genitive Case (review)

Acrescenta-se:

' aos substantivos terminados em *s*:
The boy**s'** book is new.

's aos substantivos não terminados em *s*:
The boy**'s** book is old.

Whose?: De quem?

Whose pen is that?
It's Mary's.

Whose shoes are those?
They're the girls'.

8 Answer the questions.

1 Whose book is this? (Peter)
It's Peter's.

2 Is this your kite? (no / Marian)
No. It's Marian's.

3 Are those my records? (no / the teachers)
____

4 Is this your magazine? (no / Roberta)
____

5 Whose colored pencils are those? (the kids)
____

6 Whose bags are those? (Mom)
____

9 Rewrite the sentences. Use the Genitive Case.

1 Those are the pens of the students.
Those are the students' pens.

2 This is the address of Tessa.
____

3 Where are the keys of the drivers?
____

4 Is that the wife of Mr. Gordon?
____

5 The pen of the doctor is on the table.
____

6 That is the book of Pat.
____

GRAMMAR

Possessive Adjectives and Pronouns

Possessive Adjectives	Possessive Pronouns
my	mine
your	yours
his	his
her	hers
its	its
our	ours
your	yours
their	theirs

A concordância do *Possessive Adjective* ou do *Possessive Pronoun* é feita com o possuidor.

I wash **my** hands.

Possessive Adjective

She washes **hers**.

***Possessive Pronoun** = her hands*

10 Complete the sentences. Use Possessive Adjectives or Possessive Pronouns.

1 I like *my* school. Do you like *yours*?

2 Those girls always bring ____________ books. Those boys never bring ____________.

3 Joe, is this ____________ pen? "Joe" is written on it.

4 **A:** What's your name?

B: ____________ name is Susan, and ____________?

A: ____________ is Jessica.

5 **A:** Did Peter wash ____________ own bike yesterday?

B: Yes, he did. And Susan washed ____________, too.

6 **A:** Dan, is this ____________ pencil case?

B: No, it isn't. ____________ is here.

11 Write sentences. Use Possessive Pronouns.

1 This is not Martin's jacket.

He wants his.

2 This is not Katy's pen.

____

3 This is not Joseph's guitar.

____

4 This is not the girls' dictionary.

____

5 These are not our CDs.

____

6 Those are not my pens.

____

12 Look at the picture. Then listen to the sentences and check the chart. There is only one object for each teenager.

	MARY	SALLY	CARLA	DEAN	DAVID	JACK
bike						
book						
cat						
dog						
skateboard						
tablet						

13 Read the messages. Then write your message to the students of Hiroshima.

I'll write peace on your wings and you'll fly all over the world.

Sadako Sasaki, age 12

To the students of Hiroshima,

I read Sadako's history.

We, the students of the 21st century, have to protest against atomic bombs.

I am sending a paper crane that I folded. Please put it in Sadako's monument.

Eduardo Castro e Silva, age 13

FUN

14 Let's fold a paper crane?

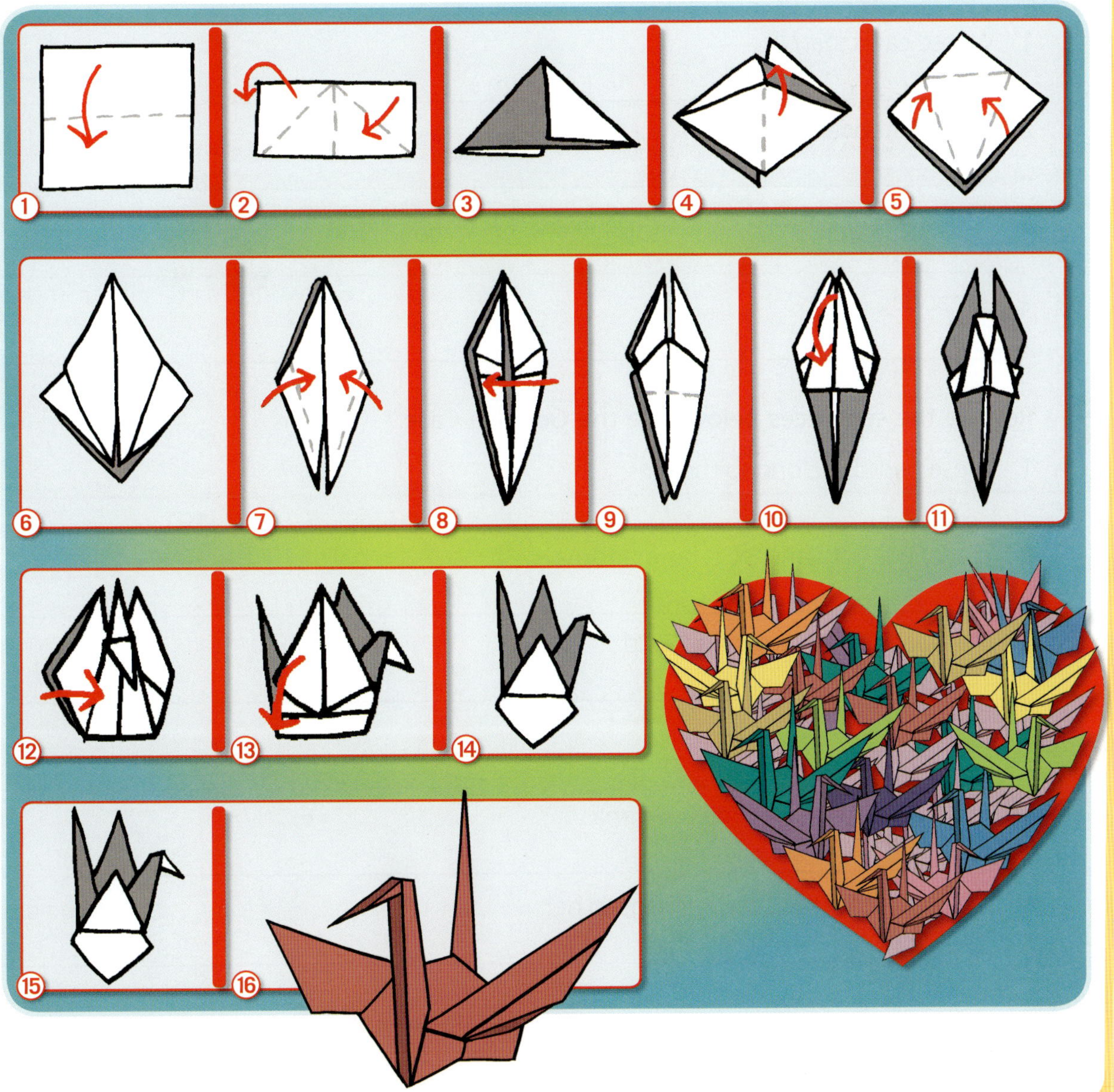

Key Language

7

crane	drop	lively	slight
deadly	fold	pain	square
disease	fund	race	survive
dizziness	healthy	raise	symptom

Way to Go

1 Answer the questions below based on the picture in exercise 12, on page 23.

1 Whose cat is that?

____

2 Is the skateboard Dean's?

____

3 Whose tablet is that?

____

4 Is that dog Mary's?

____

2 Rewrite the sentences below. Use the Genitive Case.

1 Those pencils belong to the girls.

____

2 That's Leo. Mrs. Sanchez is his grandma.

____

3 That's Jack. Catherine is his friend.

____

4 That dog belongs to Michael.

____

5 This is my sister. Her name is Helena.

____

6 This is Martha. That book belongs to her.

____

3 Complete the conversations. Use the appropriate pronoun.

1 **A:** Is that your skateboard?

B: Of course it's *mine*. I got it from *my* uncle.

2 **A:** Is that Ana's doll?

B: Of course it's ___________. She got it from ___________ aunt.

3 **A:** Is that the boys' kite?

B: Of course it's ___________. They got it from ___________ parents.

4 **A:** Is that Gabriel's truck?

B: Of course it's ___________. He got it from ___________ mother.

5 **A:** Are those our CDs?

B: Of course they're ___________. We got them from ___________ grandpa.

4 Read the text about The Children's Peace Monument. Then underline:

1 a verb that corresponds to lament 2 a precious metal 3 a reward

The Children's Peace Monument

The Children's Peace Monument is also called the "Tower of a Thousand Cranes", for many thousands of folded paper cranes are offered there all through the year. [...]

Shocked by Sadako's death, her classmates put out a national call to build a monument to mourn all the children who died from the atomic bombing. With the support of students from more than 3,100 schools around Japan and in nine other countries [...], the Society was able to build this bronze statue that stands nine meters high.[...]

Inscribed on the stone underneath the pedestal is "This is our cry. This is our prayer. For building peace in this world."

The monument was created by Kazuo Kikuchi, then a professor of Fine Arts and Music at Tokyo University. A gold crane [...] was initially hung under a bell inside the tower. This piece was contributed by Dr. Hideki Yukawa, winner of the Nobel Prize for Physics [...]. It was made as a wind chime.

Extracted from: <www.city.hiroshima.lg.jp>. Accessed on: April 11, 2012.

5 Order the following events according to the text.

- [ ] Sadako died.
- [ ] The Children's Peace Monument was created by Kazuo Kikuchi.
- [ ] A bomb was dropped in Japan.
- [ ] Dr. Hideki Yukawa made a new piece for the monument.

6 Read the text again. Then answer the questions below.

1 How many countries were involved in the building of Children's Peace Monument?

____

2 What's the height of the monument?

____

3 What does the monument represent to the Japanese people?

____

4 Dr. Hideki Yukawa was one of the winners of the Nobel Prize for Physics. Do you know any other categories of Nobel Prize?

____

3 The Lady in the Cave

1 Answer.

1 Do you always tell the truth?

2 Imagine the truth is a person. What does she look like?

8 **2** Read this story about the truth.

The Lady in the Cave

Once upon a time there was a very successful man. He had almost everything: a good wife, a nice family and a beautiful house. However, he felt unhappy. One day, he told his wife, "I am not happy. I have to know Truth."

"Then," she answered, "go look for her. It is something you should do for yourself."

The man asked his wife to take care of their family and possessions, and went out to search for Truth.

He traveled miles and miles. He walked across forests and deserts and sailed the seven seas. He asked people about Truth in towns, villages, valleys and mountains. He looked for Truth for many days, many weeks, many months. Then one day, following some information, he found her in a very small cave, on the top of a distant mountain.

Truth was a thin woman and looked very, very old. Her skin was dried and her hair was long and white. She had a long nose and only one tooth left in her mouth.

The man was paralyzed!

Then she spoke, and her voice was so beautiful that the man felt immediately happy.

She talked to him about many things he didn't know.

Then she said, "Your time is over. You have to leave."

"My lady Truth, I left my wife, my family, and my friends to learn from you," he said. "Now I must go back home. However I know I cannot think of myself only. Is there anything I can do for you? Just tell me!"

Truth looked at the man for a long time and said, "If people ask about me, tell them I look young and beautiful."

15

Based on: <www.donnajacobsife.com>. Accessed on: May 11, 2012.

3 Check the correct alternative.

1 This text is:

a ☐ a fable.
b ☐ a folk tale.
c ☐ a magazine article.

2 This text is:

a ☐ probably very old and passed from generation to generation.
b ☐ a typical internet text.
c ☐ a true story.

3 The author of this text is probably:

a ☐ from England.
b ☐ unknown.
c ☐ a famous writer.

4 According to the text, write T (true) or F (false).

1 ☐ The man was unhappy because he was poor.
2 ☐ He found Truth only after a long time.
3 ☐ Truth was not a beautiful woman.
4 ☐ Truth asked the man to tell a lie.

5 Find in the text a sentence that tells us Truth was generous to the man.

___

6 Find in the box the synonyms for the underlined words. Write them.

belongings	finished	nearly	seek

1 "Your time is over" ___
2 "He had almost everything" ___
3 "Go look for her" ___
4 "The man asked his wife to take care of their family and possessions" ___

Let's Talk about It

A história "The Lady in the Cave" nos mostra que a verdade não é bonita. Você concorda? Você acha que a verdade, às vezes, pode machucar? Por que a verdade pede ao homem que ele diga às pessoas que ela é jovem e bonita?

GRAMMAR

Should

Affirmative:	He **should** invite me.	*Should* (deve, deveria) é usado para expressar um conselho:
Negative:	He **should not** invite me. **shouldn't**	You look sick. You **should** see a doctor. People **shouldn't** waste water.
Interrogative:	**Should** he invite me?	
Short answers:	Yes, he **should**. No, he **shouldn't**.	

7 Write sentences. Use *should*.

1 

Bob's bedroom is messy.

He should clean his bedroom.

2 

Kelly can't speak out loud because she has a sore throat.

____

3 

I have a very important Math test tomorrow.

____

4 

The boy is very tired because he woke up very early.

____

5 

Jenny doesn't like the clothes she has to go to the party.

____

GRAMMAR

Reflexive Pronouns

Subjective Pronouns	Reflexive Pronouns
I	my**self**
you	your**self**
he	him**self**
she	her**self**
it	it**self**
we	our**selves**
you	your**selves**
they	them**selves**

O *Reflexive Pronoun* é geralmente usado quando o sujeito e o objeto da oração são a mesma pessoa. A concordância é feita com o sujeito.

I looked at **myself** in the mirror.
We cut **ourselves** on the old gate.

Observação: *by* + *Reflexive Pronoun* = alone
The boy made the cake **by himself**.

8 Match the columns to complete the sentences.

1 The boys hurt ______________ when they were playing tennis.
2 I'll give ______________ a beautiful necklace.
3 After the game, we bought ______________ some sandwiches.
4 Sue, Jack! Behave ______________.
5 The old man called ______________ a genius.
6 The dog found the way back by ______________.
7 Bob! You have to do your homework by ______________.

a ☐ myself
b ☐ ourselves
c ☐ itself
d ☐ yourself
e ☐ yourselves
f ☐ himself
g ☐ themselves

9 Fill in the blanks. Use the correct Reflexive Pronouns.

1 Joanne looked at *herself* in the mirror and smiled.
2 Come on, you guys! Behave ______________!
3 My mother always talks to ______________ when she is alone.
4 My brother bought ______________ a new bike. It's a really good one.
5 I usually talk to ______________ when I have a problem.
6 The girls hurt ______________ in the park.
7 Patrick, look at ______________. You are terribly dirty.
8 That dog hurt ______________ in the backyard.
9 We can't wash ______________ with this dirty water.
10 My father gave ______________ a new car.

9 **10** Listen to the sentences and number the correct picture.

1

2

3

4

5

6

7

8

11 Practice the dialogue with a classmate.

1

The kitchen is a mess.
(Do the dishes)

A: *The kitchen is a mess.*

B: *You should do the dishes.*

2

Sheila is bored. (Talk to her)

3

It's very cold today.
(Close the window)

4

It's raining heavily.
(Go by car)

12 Talk to a classmate. Use *by* and a Reflexive Pronoun.

1

you / carry this box

A: *Do you need help?*

B: *Yes, I can't carry this box by myself.*

2

they / clean that room

3

she / open the door

4

you / do the exercise

5

he / change the wheel

13 Complete the sentences with *should* and the expressions from the box.

brush our teeth	eat	say "good morning"
say "hello"	wash our hands	

1 When we get up, we *should say "good morning"* to our parents.
2 When we meet our friends, we ______________________________.
3 After we use the toilet, we ______________________________.
4 We ______________________________ after eating.
5 We ______________________________ if we are not hungry.

14 Write a composition about telling lies. Have you ever told one? Why? What were the consequences?

FUN

15 Play word battle with a classmate.

INSTRUCTIONS

1 Write five words (with four letters or more) on your chart.

2 Don't cross the words. Look at the example.

Example: w / h o u s e / r / k

3 Listen to your teacher's instruction now.

4 Play the game with a classmate.

YOU

	A	B	C	D	E	F	G	H	I	J
1										
2										
3										
4										
5										
6										
7										
8										
9										
10										

YOUR CLASSMATE

	A	B	C	D	E	F	G	H	I	J
1										
2										
3										
4										
5										
6										
7										
8										
9										
10										

10 **Key Language**

cave	mouth	search	tooth
lady	nose	skin	truth

Way to Go

1 Rewrite the sentences below and correct all Reflexive Pronouns.

1 Poor Lucy! She got desperate when she saw himself in trouble.

____

2 Behave yourself, children!

____

3 The dog found its way home by themselves.

____

4 I'm going crazy. I'm always talking to ourselves.

____

5 My sisters love looking at herself in the mirror.

____

2 Look at the pictures and complete the sentences. Use *should* or *shouldn't*.

1

They ______________ feed the animals. It's dangerous.

2

Albert is a little chubby. He ______________ eat so much pizza.

3

You're always sleepy. You ______________ go to bed earlier every day.

4

Rex is very dirty. You ______________ wash your dog.

3 Write sentences about the people in the pictures below. Use *should* and the cues from the box.

drink some hot tea with honey and lemon — drink some water — get some rest — go out with her friends

1

Peter / thirsty

Peter is thirsty. He should drink some water.

2

Julia / cold

____

____

3

Paul and John / very tired

____

____

4

Samantha / bored

____

____

11 **4** Listen to some dos and don'ts for job interviews. Then check the correct alternative.

1 You should dress
- a ☐ formal clothes.
- b ☐ professionally.
- c ☐ casual clothes.

2 You should bring
- a ☐ a pen and a pencil.
- b ☐ one résumé.
- c ☐ a pen and extra copies of your résumé.

3 You should arrive
- a ☐ 5 to 10 minutes before.
- b ☐ 10 to 15 minutes before.
- c ☐ 15 to 30 minutes before.

4 You should behave
- a ☐ in a rude way.
- b ☐ in a defensive way.
- c ☐ in an honest way.

Audio extracted from: <www.youtube.com>. Accessed on: May 9, 2012.

4 Have You Ever Seen the Rain?

1 Answer.

1 What kind of text is this?

2 How do you know?

12 **2** Read the lyrics and listen to the song.

Have You Ever Seen the Rain?

Creedence Clearwater Revival

Someone told me long ago
There's a calm before the storm
I know,
It's been comin' for some time.
When it's over, so they say
It'll rain a sunny day
I know; shinin' down like water.

I want to know
Have you ever seen the rain?
I want to know
Have you ever seen the rain?
Comin' down on a sunny day?

Yesterday and days before
Sun is cold and rain is hard
I know; been that way for all my time.
'Till forever, on it goes
Through the circle, fast and slow,
I know, it can't stop, I wonder.

I want to know
Have you ever seen the rain?
I want to know
Have you ever seen the rain?
Comin' down on a sunny day?

Yeah!

I want to know
Have you ever seen the rain?
I want to know
Have you ever seen the rain?
Comin' down on a sunny day?

Extracted from: <www.lyrics.com>. Accessed on: June 10, 2012.

3 Underline pairs of rhyming words in the verses below.

When it's over, so they say

It'll rain a sunny day

I know; shinin' down like water.

4 Look for the words below in the glossary. Write their translations.

1 someone ______________________

2 long ago ______________________

3 calm ______________________

4 storm ______________________

5 rain ______________________

6 sunny ______________________

5 Read the lyrics again and write T (true) or F (false).

The day before...

1 [ ] it rained.

2 [ ] it was sunny and cold.

3 [ ] it was hot.

4 [ ] there was a storm.

6 What did you understand when you read the following verses? Answer in Portuguese.

1 "There's a calm before the storm."

____

2 "It's been comin' for some time."

____

Let's Talk about It

Muitas vezes, os sentimentos e as experiências apresentados em músicas e canções não são de seus compositores, e sim do eu-lírico. Por que, então, as pessoas escrevem esses tipos de texto? E por que as pessoas gostam de músicas e poemas?

GRAMMAR

Present Perfect

I / You — **have seen** him. ('ve)
He / She / It — **has seen** him. ('s)
We / You / They — **have seen** him. ('ve)

Negative: I **have not** seen him. (**haven't**)
She **has not** seen him. (**hasn't**)

Interrogative: **Have** you **seen** him?

Short answers: Yes, I **have**.
No, I **haven't**.

O *Present Perfect* expressa uma ação que aconteceu em um tempo não definido no passado. Ele é formado por *have/has* seguido do particípio passado do verbo principal.

7 Complete the sentences. Use the Present Perfect.

1 I *have been* (be) to Spain.
2 He ________________ (see) a ghost.
3 She ________________ (find) her keys.
4 They ________________ (go) to the recreational club.
5 We ________________ (live) by the lake.
6 I ________________ (walk) to school.

INFINITIVE	SIMPLE PAST	PAST PARTICIPLE
be	was/were	been
do	did	done
find	found	found
go	went	gone
see	saw	seen
sell	sold	sold
send	sent	sent
think	thought	thought

8 Match the questions to their answers.

1 Have they been to Paris?
2 Where have you been?
3 Has he found his tablet?
4 What has she sold?
5 Where has Mr. Green lived?
6 Have you thought about your life?
7 What have they seen?
8 Has she baked a cake?

a [ ] They have seen a car accident.
b [ ] He has lived in São Paulo and Brasília.
c [*1*] Yes, they have.
d [ ] No, I haven't
e [ ] No, he hasn't.
f [ ] Yes, she has.
g [ ] She's sold her house.
h [ ] I've been to the park.

9 Look at the pictures. Then practice the dialogues with a classmate. Use the cues given.

1

clean the kitchen

A: What has she done?

B: *She's cleaned the kitchen.*

2

yes

A: Have they been to France?

B: *Yes, they have. / Yep.*

3

no

A: Has he sold his motorbike?

B: *No, he hasn't. / Nope.*

4

paint the gate

5

no

6

play tennis

7

send an e-mail

8

yes

9

no

13 **10** Listen to the poem. Write the missing words.

The Sun and the Moon

Elisabeth Prescher

Hello, said the Sun,
Where have you been?
Hi, said the ______,
I've been spinning around!
Then tell me exactly
What you have ______.

I've seen ______ beaches,
I've listened to secrets,
I've ______ sleepy fields,
I've kissed silent valleys,
I've touched dormant ______,
I've ______ on silver lakes!

Oh, C'mon, said the Sun,
I am the ______,
Where are all those ______
That I haven't seen?

Well, well, said the Moon,
Though you have the light,
Magic things, my Lord,
Happen under the ______!

11 Answer the questions according to the poem.

1 Who is involved in the conversation?

______

2 The Sun thinks he is more important than the Moon. And the Moon thinks she is more important. Find two sentences that show each of these situations.

______

12 Look at the pictures again. Which one best illustrates the poem? Check.

GRAMMAR

Present Perfect *versus* Simple Past

Present Perfect
Expressa uma ação que ocorreu no passado, porém sem que seja determinado o momento exato em que isso aconteceu.
We **have lived** in Europe.

Expressa uma ação que foi iniciada em um momento no passado e ainda não terminou.
She **has traveled** a lot lately.

Simple Past
Expressa uma ação que ocorreu em um tempo determinado no passado.
We **lived** in Europe last year.
She **traveled** last month.

13 Complete the sentences with the verbs in parentheses. Use the Simple Past or the Present Perfect.

1 My grandparents *sold* (sell) their car last week.
2 The teacher ______________ (tell) us a beautiful story.
3 ______________ you ______________ (see) Andy yesterday?
4 ______________ you ______________ (see) Tom in the last two days?
5 The boys ______________ (be) in the park an hour ago.
6 I ______________ (find – neg.) my keys last night.
7 My sister ______________ (work) there since 2010.
8 How much money ______________ you ______________ (spend) last week?

14 Answer the questions about yourself.

1 Where did you go yesterday?
____
2 Who did you see last night?
____
3 Did you have a sandwich yesterday?
____
4 What have you bought recently?
____
5 What have you studied for your exams?
____
6 Have you ever met your classmates out of school?
____

15 Complete the lyrics with words that rhyme. Use the ones from the box.

dragonfly	degrees	fun	high
please	seas	sky	stars	sun

Fly Away
Lenny Kravitz

I wish that I could fly
Into the ________
So very ________
Just like a ________

I'd fly above the trees
Over the ________
In all ________
To anywhere I ________

Oh I want to get away
I want to fly away
Yeah yeah yeah

Let's go and see the ________
The Milky Way or even Mars
Where it could just be ours

Let's fade into the ________
Let your spirit fly
Where we are one
Just for a little ________
Oh oh oh yeah!

I want to get away
I want to fly away
Yeah yeah yeah

Extracted from: <www.lyrics.com>.
Accessed on: May 10, 2012.

FUN

16 Create a word search. Write the Past Participle of the verbs below in the grid. Then complete the boxes with the alphabet letters.

IRREGULAR VERBS

be	feel	see
break	find	sell
do	go	think

REGULAR VERBS

believe	kiss	look
carry	listen	study
climb	live	touch

Key Language

14

calm	fast	rain	storm
cold	forever	shine	sunny
come	hard	slow	through
down	like	so	wonder
ever	long ago	someone	

Way to Go

1 Change the sentences into the required form.

1 Chris has finished her work. (interrogative)

____

2 Grandpa has told them a story. (negative)

____

3 They have sold their car. (negative)

____

4 We have studied hard. (interrogative)

____

5 Peter hasn't washed his bike. (affirmative)

____

2 Underline the correct alternative.

1 My friend and I **went** / **have gone** to the movies yesterday.

2 **Did** / **Have** they read the newspaper recently?

3 I **saw** / **have seen** those boys last week.

4 The class **finished** / **has finished** 20 minutes ago.

3 Complete the questions for the following answers.

1 What *did he have yesterday*?

He had a headache yesterday.

2 Who ____?

She saw her best friend last night.

3 What ____?

Mom has bought a lot of clothes.

4 Where ____?

They lived in France two years ago.

5 Where ____?

She's gone to the theater.

6 How ____?

He's gone to school by bus.

4 Listen to the phone conversation between Priscilla and Amanda. Complete it with the appropriate verb.

Priscilla: Hello, Amanda.

Amanda: Hi, Priscilla. How are you?

Priscilla: I'm fine. What about you?

Amanda: I'm OK. Listen. ________________ you ________________ about U2's concert at the HZ Arena?

Priscilla: Sure! And I really ________________ to go. It's my favorite band, you know. Do you know how much the tickets are?

Amanda: Unfortunately not. I ________________ to call the organizers yesterday, but nobody ________________ the phone.

Priscilla: I see. What about accessing their website? Have you ________________ that?

Amanda: I ________________ it some time ago, but there is no information there.

Priscilla: Oh, Gosh...

Amanda: But I have an idea!

Priscilla: Tell me.

Amanda: Why don't we go to the HZ Arena and get all the information we need?

Priscilla: OK, then.

Amanda: I'm coming to your place to pick you up.

Priscilla: Wait, wait, wait. I ________________ just ________________ a shower and I still have to finish drying my hair.

Amanda: All right. See you then.

Priscilla: See you!

5 Read the phone conversation in the exercise above. Write T (true) or F (false).

1 ☐ Amanda has heard about U2's concert.
2 ☐ It's the first time Priscilla has heard about the concert.
3 ☐ The organizers website has all the information the girls need.
4 ☐ Amanda has accepted Priscilla's suggestion of going to the HZ Arena.
5 ☐ Priscila took a shower some minutes before the phone call.

5 The Twins

1 Answer the questions.

1 Have you ever seen street art? What is it?

2 Are street artists famous?

16 **2** Read the interview with two Brazilian street artists.

Interview Os Gêmeos

Os Gêmeos, or The Twins, are two twin brothers from São Paulo, Brazil. They are the street artists Otavio and Gustavo Pandolfo. In recent years, they have gained international fame for their incredible painting work on the streets. Their works use latex, rollers and spray for the details, among other materials.

Our Way: How long have you both been painting?

Os Gêmeos: We have been painting since 1986.

OW: What other countries have you painted in?

OG: Many countries... Argentina, Chile, Uruguay, Puerto Rico, Cuba, the U.S., Canada, Portugal, Spain, France, Germany, Austria, Italy, Lithuania, Russia, England, Scotland, Greece, Japan, China and a few more...

OW: Who influences your art?

OG: A lot of things influence us: life, arts, dreams, food, family, trips, graffiti, nature, friends, love, hatred, music, drums, DJs, the 1930s, different artists and singers, exhibits, World War II, Lithuania, etc.

OW: Do you think your art belongs to a Brazilian movement or to a global movement?

OG: To the global movement. It's a major movement nowadays.

OW: Where have you had the most exciting experience?

OG: We believe that every work is exciting. There is something special in every work, even small works. Everything is part of the whole... where everything is connected.

OW: What is your favorite food?

OG: That's very difficult to say, but rice, potatoes, Japanese, Italian, and Lithuanian food are some of our favorites.

An exclusive interview kindly granted by the artists Otavio and Gustavo Pandolfo, Os Gêmeos, published for the first time in *Our Way 4*, Premium Edition.

3 Find in the text the opposite of the underlined words.

1 We have been to <u>many</u> countries. ________________

2 A lot of things have influenced our art: life, art, <u>love</u>, etc. ________________

4 Check the correct alternative.

1 The word "both" in the text refers to:

- [ ] one person
- [ ] two people
- [ ] more than two people

2 The word "drums" refers to:

- [ ] a musical instrument
- [ ] a kind of food
- [ ] a kind of drink

5 Write T (true) or F (false) according to the text.

1 ( ) Otavio and Gustavo are famous only in Brazil.

2 ( ) They like only Brazilian food.

3 ( ) Different things influence their work.

4 ( ) They have been painting for more than 25 years.

6 Answer the questions.

1 Is it the first time the interview is published?

____

2 What kind of material do they use in their work?

____

3 What influences their art?

____

____

____

Let's Talk about It

Tornar a arte acessível é importante para aproximar a população da cultura do país, de forma geral. O que você pensa a respeito?

GRAMMAR

Present Perfect: Adverbs (Since, For, Ever, Never)

Since (desde) é usado para indicar o início de uma ação:
I have been here **since** 9 o'clock.

For (por) é usado para indicar um período específico:
I have lived here **for** 10 years.

Ever (alguma vez) é usado em perguntas.
Have you **ever** seen that movie?

Never (nunca) é usado em frases negativas com verbos na forma afirmativa.
I have **never** been to that place.

7 Complete the sentences with *since*, *for*, *ever* or *never*.

1 I have worked there *for* a year.
2 We have studied Spanish ______________ three years.
3 He has lived here ______________ January.
4 She has ______________ been to Rio.
5 Have you ______________ talked to that famous artist?
6 They have talked ______________ three hours.
7 I have ______________ written a letter.
8 Have they ______________ been to your house?

8 Rewrite the sentences. Use the words in parentheses.

1 I have lived abroad. (never)
I have never lived abroad.
2 Your sister has been to London. (ever)
____
3 He hasn't seen Karen. (since last month)
____
4 We have been at Grandma's house. (for two hours)
____
5 Mr. and Mrs. Oliver have visited my family. (never)
____
6 Jack has eaten chocolate. (ever)
____

9 Look at the pictures. Then practice the dialogues with a classmate.

1

chocolate bar / eat

2

the medicine / take

3

the car key / lose

A: *Where's the chocolate bar?*
B: *She's just eaten it.*

4

the sandwich / eat

5

the ice cream / have

6

the composition / lose

INFINITIVE	SIMPLE PAST	PAST PARTICIPLE
bring	brought	brought
eat	ate	eaten
lose	lost	lost
make	made	made
read	read	read
take	took	taken
write	wrote	written

10 Talk to a classmate. Use the sentences given.

1 Do your homework, please.
A: *Do your homework, please.*
B: *I've already done it.*
A: *When did you do it?*
B: *I did it five minutes ago.*

2 Make me a sandwich, please.
3 Bring me a glass of water, please.
4 Write our shopping list, please.
5 Read the instructions, please.
6 Clean your bedroom, please.

GRAMMAR

Present Perfect: Adverbs (Just, Already, Yet, Lately)

Just (acabar de) é usado ao se referir a uma ação que aconteceu pouco tempo antes do momento em que se fala.
The plane has **just** arrived.

Already (já) é usado em perguntas e frases afirmativas.
She has **already** done the exercises.

Yet (já, ainda não) é usado em perguntas e frases negativas.
Has the baby slept **yet**?
The baby has not slept **yet**.

Lately (ultimamente) é usado ao se referir a uma ação que tem acontecido com frequência.
I've worked hard **lately**.

11 Rewrite the sentences. Use the cues given.

1 They found their dog. (just)
They've just found their dog.

2 She has studied History. (yet – int.)
____

3 They've written the composition. (yet – neg.)
____

4 We have done our homework. (already – aff.)
____

5 Your brother has arrived. (just)
____

12 Answer the questions about yourself.

1 Have you ever been to the desert? Where?
____

2 Have you ever seen a penguin? Where?
____

3 How long have you lived in the same house/apartment?
____

4 Have you ever helped a person on the street? Who?
____

5 Can you mention a place you have never been to but want to visit? What place?
____

6 Can you mention a place you have never been to and don't want to visit? What place?
____

13 Listen to the dialogues. Then number the pictures.

14 Read some questions that can be asked in interviews. Then, add two more questions.

- What's your favorite food?
- What's your favorite song?
- What's your favorite activity?
- What do you like doing?
- What do you hate doing?
- What's your favorite time of day?
- What's your favorite period of the year?
- What was one of the best days you've ever had?
- Do you have a favorite movie or book?
- What's the best and the worst gift you've ever received?
- When was the last time you got angry?
- How did you start your career?
- What do you do every day?
- How many hours do you work a day?
- Do you have brothers/sisters/children?
- Have you ever been to (name of a place)?
- What countries/cities have you visited?

15 Write some questions to ask to a classmate. Then, interview him/her. Write down the answers.

FUN

16 Play tic-tac-toe.

- Have you ever seen a ghost?
- How much did your book cost?
- What did you read last week?
- Have you read *Romeo and Juliet*?
- Have you ever lost your keys?
- Do you usually tell lies?
- Have you ever told a lie?
- Where did you go last Sunday?
- Do you often go to parties?
- What do you like to eat?
- Have you ever had an accident?
- What is there in your bag?
- What person do you like most?
- Who's your best friend?
- Do you help the people at home?
- Who helps you when you need help?
- Can you cook?
- Who's your favorite singer?
- What's your favorite song?

Grid 1

Grid 2

TOTAL SCORE

YOU	YOUR CLASSMATE

18

Key Language

arts
dream
drums
exciting
fame
graffiti
hatred
influence
interview
latex
paint
roller
spray
street artist
twins

Way to Go

1 Check the best alternative. Then complete the sentences.

1 I've studied at this school ________________ 2010.
a ☐ for b ☐ since c ☐ just

2 She's worked at that company ________________ 3 years.
a ☐ already b ☐ for c ☐ since

3 Have you ________________ been to Los Angeles?
a ☐ yet b ☐ since c ☐ ever

4 They have ________________ seen that movie, but they want to.
a ☐ never b ☐ just c ☐ since

5 The classes have ________________ finished. But the children are still inside the school.
a ☐ already b ☐ yet c ☐ for

2 Unscramble the words to form sentences.

1 have / They / finished / homework / already / their / .
____

2 yet / train / hasn't / The / arrived / .
____

3 you / Have / been / there / ever / ?
____

4 has / since / 2011 / abroad / lived / She / .
____

5 never / I / Japan / have / visited / .
____

3 Go back to page 52. Ask the questions from exercise 12 to a classmate and write his/her answers below.

1 ____
2 ____
3 ____
4 ____
5 ____
6 ____

4 Complete the e-mail Janice has written to her friend Chris. Use the words from the box.

have – been	have brought	have – come	have – seen
	have seen	have stayed	

To: chris@ow.com
Subject: London

Send | Attach

Hi, Chris, R U OK?

I'm pretty good!

I ______________ just ______________ back from London and I'm really astonished. That city is amazing, dude! You've got to go there.

I saw so many interesting tourist attractions like I ______________ never ______________ before: Big Ben, The London Eye, The Houses of Parliament! But there's one thing that really made me crazy: Madame Tussauds! It's a wax museum that you can find in many places in the world. ______________ you ever ______________ to one?

It's so interesting that I ______________________ there for more than 3 hours. Just AMAZING, like almost everything I saw in that city.

I ______________________ a tourist folder from there. Find it attached.

You can also access www.madametussauds.com/London/Default.aspx and see everything I ______________.

Write me back asap, OK?

Jan

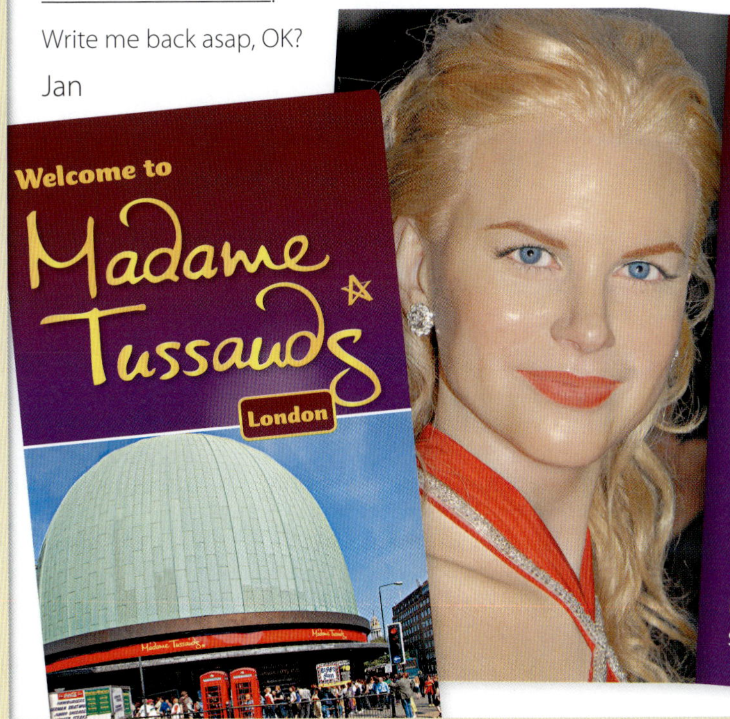

Madame Tussauds is a museum that contains wax models of famous people. There are numerous galleries such as Pirates of the Caribbean, World Leaders, The Royal Family, Sports Stars, the Culture Zone and the History of London.

You can have your picture taken alongside A-list celebrities like Drew Barrymore, Orlando Bloom, Nicole Kidman and Leonardo DiCaprio.

The Music Zone represents legends of pop from Bob Marley through to current chart toppers Kylie and Justin Timberlake. Visitors are encouraged to try out their own dance moves to see if they can win an award.

Extracted from: <www.tourist-information-uk.com>. Accessed on May 7, 2012.

6 War Horse: from the Book to the Screen

1 Answer the following questions.

1 What kind of movies do you prefer?

2 Have you ever seen any movies or read any books about wars?

19 **2** Read the following texts.

Address: www.amazon.com Find

The Book

Joey, a beautiful horse with a white cross on his nose, is sold to the cavalry and shipped to France to go to the war. The fighting is chaotic and he witnesses the horror of the battles in France. Joey is always sad thinking about Albert, his true master who is left behind. The horse has a deep bond with his young master, who embarks on a dangerous mission to find the animal and bring him back to Devon, in southwestern England. Will the horse ever see his true master again?

Based on: <www.amazon.com>. Accessed on: May 8, 2012.

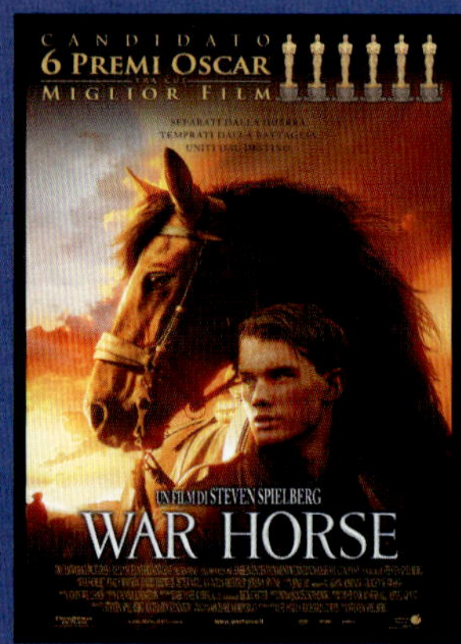

The Movie *War Horse*

Production year: 2011
Country: U.S.
Runtime: 146 min.
Director: Steven Spielberg
Cast: Benedict Cumberbatch, David Thewlis, Emily Watson, Jeremy Irvine, Niels Arestrup, Peter Mullan, Toby Kebbell, Tom Hiddleston

Based on: <http://interfilmes.com>; <www.imdb.com>. Accessed on: May 8, 2012.

Behind the Scenes

War Horse, a drama film directed by Steven Spielberg, is set before and during World War I.
The shoot for the movie, which is based on a children's book by Michael Morpurgo, used 5,800 extras, 300 horses, and a team of 750 people who dug over 250 yards of trenches.
Work on the trenches took six weeks. Spielberg filmed the scenes in one month, in October of 2010, and the typically British weather meant the actors had to film in trenches filled with water. "It was freezing and raining," said the producer Kathleen Kennedy.
The main village scenes were shot in Castle Combe, England, over 100 miles from Dartmoor, the author's home village.
Critics who have seen the film said the scenes of the Battle of Somme, in France, are as realistic as the opening of Spielberg's *Saving Private Ryan*.

Based on: <www.guardian.co.uk>; <www.telegraph.co.uk>. Accessed on: May 8, 2012.

3 Write T (true) or F (false), according to the texts.

1 [ ] Joey is the name of a boy in the movie.
2 [ ] The movie was filmed in England.
3 [ ] The book was written by Michael Morpurgo.
4 [ ] Steven Spielberg is a movie director.

4 Go to the glossary at the end of the book. Look up the meaning of the following words related to war.

1 battle ____________________
2 soldier ____________________
3 army ____________________
4 trench ____________________

5 Read the texts again. Find:

1 an expression that best describes the relationship between Albert and Joey:

____

2 two words that describe the "typical British weather":

____

3 a word that best describes the genre of the movie *War Horse*:

____

6 Answer these questions according to the texts.

1 How long did it take to shoot the village scenes?

____

2 In what country did the Battle of Somme take place?

____

3 The text compares *War Horse* to another movie directed by Steven Spielberg. What movie was it?

____

Let's Talk about It

Na história da humanidade, sempre houve interação entre o homem e o animal. Nessa relação, qual é a parte mais frágil? Por quê?

GRAMMAR

Relative Pronouns: Who (That) / Where

Relative Pronouns são usados para unir duas orações. Podem substituir um pronome ou um substantivo.

Who (que, o(s) qual(is), a(s) qual(is)) refere-se a pessoas. Pode ser substituído por *that*:
The men are my neighbors. They saw the accident.

The men [**who** / **that**] saw the accident are my neighbors.

Where (onde, em que) refere-se a lugares:
He is at the restaurant. We have lunch at that restaurant.
He is at the restaurant **where** we have lunch.

7 Complete the sentences with *who* or *where*.

1 This is the city *where* she lives.
2 Mr. Clever is the person ________________ was looking at you.
3 I usually don't go to places ________________ there are many people.
4 Joan and I talked to the man ________________ was playing the guitar.
5 Michael loves the girl ________________ lives near his house.
6 A supermarket is a place ________________ we can buy food.
7 Those are the boys ________________ I met yesterday.

8 Write sentences about people and places. Use the cues given.

1 the garden / the place / my dogs sleep
The garden is the place where my dogs sleep.
2 a pilot / a person / flies airplanes
A pilot is a person who flies airplanes. / A pilot is a person that flies airplanes.
3 a kitchen / the place / we eat
____
4 a living room / the place / we watch TV
____
5 this girl / the person / help me
____
6 the mechanic / the person / fix cars
____

GRAMMAR

Relative Pronouns: Which (That) / Whose

Which (que, o(s) qual(is), a(s) qual(is)) refere-se a coisas ou a animais. Pode ser substituído por *that*:
Whales are animals. Whales live in the sea.

Whales are animals [**which** / **that**] live in the sea.

A key is an object. It locks doors.

A key is an object [**which** / **that**] locks doors.

Whose (cujo(s), cuja(s)) indica posse:
That is my neighbor. His brother is a firefighter.
That is my neighbor **whose** brother is a firefighter.

9 Combine the sentences. Use *which*.

1 The bike is broken. It is in the garage.
The bike which is broken is in the garage. / The bike, which is in the garage, is broken.

2 A giraffe is a big animal. It eats leaves.
____

3 Mike is wearing a cap. The cap is too big for him.
____

4 That dog bit you. It has been put to sleep.
____

5 The apartment is new. The apartment is big and comfortable.
____

10 Complete the sentences with the words from the box.

where
which
who
whose

1 That's the guy __________ family went to Spain last year.
2 I love people __________ are always happy.
3 This is the place __________ I found the wallet.
4 I miss the dog __________ picture is on the wall.
5 The bike __________ is in the garage is new.
6 A balloonist is a person __________ flies balloons.
7 That is the CD player __________ battery is low.
8 The man __________ helped me yesterday is a famous actor.
9 That is the dog __________ ran after the children.
10 That is the house __________ she lives.

11 Listen to the conversation. Then check the correct alternatives.

1 How many people participate in this conversation?

a [ ] 2 b [ ] 3 c [ ] 4

2 The names of the people in the conversation are:

a [ ] Albert c [ ] Laura e [ ] Nathan g [ ] Helen

b [ ] Hannah d [ ] Linda f [ ] Jonathan h [ ] Henry

3 Where are they going to watch the ceremony?

a [ ] At Hannah's house. b [ ] At Laura's house. c [ ] At Nathan's house.

12 Listen to the people in another conversation. Then answer the questions.

1 Whose favorite movies are these?

Hugo: ____________

Harry Potter and the Deathly Hallows – Part 2: ____________

Eclipse: ____________

2 Who likes the following actors?

1

Daniel Radcliffe

____

2

Asa Butterfield

____

3 Besides *Hugo*, what other movie did Asa Butterfield star in?

____

13 Look at the pictures. Then practice the dialogues with a classmate.

1

Ted / call / Ms. Hunt

A: *Who's Ted?*

B: *He's the boy who has called Ms. Hunt.*

2

Susan / play / the violin

A: *Who's Susan?*

B: *She's the girl who has played the violin.*

3

Mike / wash / the bike

4

Lucy / paint / the wall

5
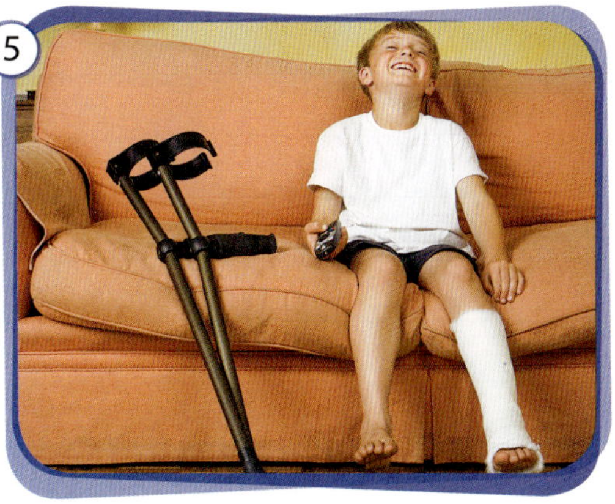

Bob / break / his leg

6

Sarah / help / the child

14 Read this book description. Then write about a book you like.

Title: *The Invention of Hugo Cabret*
Author: Brian Selznick

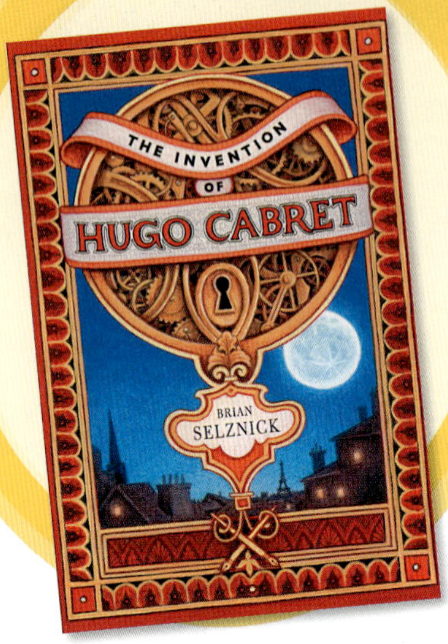

Hugo is an orphan who keeps the clocks in a Paris train station. He is secretly trying to fix a mechanical man which his father had started to build. He is convinced that the mechanical man has a message from his dead father. But when Hugo meets Isabelle and her grandfather, his life and his secret are in danger.

Based on: <www.amazon.com>. Accessed on: May 15, 2012.

Title: ______________________________

Author: ____________________________

FUN

15 Make words with the letters below.

E	S	A	N
A	P	L	E
T	K	R	C
L	I	L	F
A	H	M	Y
G	T	E	N

airplane

Key Language

army
battle
cast
freezing
shoot
trench
war
weather
yard

Way to Go

1 **Underline the correct alternative.**

1 I've just seen the woman **whose / that** son studies in my class.

2 I loved the book **which / where** I read.

3 That's the city **who / where** I go on vacation.

4 The girl **whose / who** is behind him is his sister.

2 **Choose the alternative that best completes the following book reviews.**

(1)

Title: *The Little Prince*
Author: Antoine de Saint-Exupéry

This a charming story about a little prince __________ falls to Earth from Asteroid B-612. He's a lonely little prince. He's in need of a friend, and so he sets off on a journey in __________ he will go across the planets to see the people he can find.

a ☐ who – which b ☐ where – which c ☐ who – whose

Adapted from: <www.readingmatters.co.uk>. Accessed on: May 8, 2012.

(2)

Title: *Alice's Adventures in Wonderland*
Author: Lewis Carroll

If you ever see a rabbit and follow him, like Alice, you may end up in Wonderland, the place __________ strange creatures live. There doesn't seem to be anything you can rely on, not even your own size. Alice learns how to govern her size a little by eating and drinking magic foods __________ she finds, but it is a case of trial and error.

a ☐ where – whose b ☐ who – that c ☐ where – that

Adapted from: <www.readingmatters.co.uk>. Accessed on: May 8, 2012.

3 **Rewrite the sentences below. Correct all the underlined mistakes.**

1 Lewis Carroll is the author which book is about a prince.

____

2 Alice is the girl whose follows a prince.

____

4 Write sentences. Use a word or phrase from each box.

Bob is the man She loved the gift That's the dog house The mother called the girl	where which who whose	car broke yesterday her father gave her my pet sleeps takes care of her baby

____

____

____

____

5 There are two sentences in exercise 4 that can be written with another Relative Pronoun. Rewrite them.

____

____

6 Today is Paul's first day at school. Steve is going to show everything to him. Complete the sentences he is going to use.

1

Paul will study in this classroom.

This is the classroom *where you will study*.

2

You can make copies in this room.

This is the room ______________________

______________________________.

3

Your Math teacher is going to be that woman.

That's the woman ______________________

______________________________.

4

You are going to use this book.

This is the book ______________________

______________________________.

7 Friendship

1 Answer.

1 What is a true friend?

2 Do true friends really exist?

23 **2** Read the article.

OW magazine

What Does It Mean to Be a Friend?

In the U.S., an organization dedicated to improve kids' health posted a question: What does it mean to be a friend? More than 5,000 teens expressed their opinions about it.

For many, what friends do is show their loyalty. Actions, big or small, are what really count – the friend who talks to you when you're feeling alone or the friend who camps out in your hospital room.

Most said that they do as much for their friends as their friends do for them, and they feel fine when they expect to get nothing in return.

For some, it is important to have just one best friend. For others, what is important is to have friends.

Some think communication is important, others value good judgment and honesty. Some say friendship comes with risk and responsibility. Sometimes you can trust friends and get disappointed.

It seems that romance and distance can complicate things. Some teens told of friends who had "disappeared" after they began seeing someone.

Many learned the true value of friendship after it was gone. And for some, it was OK if good friends only accompanied them for part of their life.

"People grow and change," said a girl.

14

Based on: <http://kidshealth.org>. Accessed on: May 9, 2012.

3 Read the text again. Check the sentence that can be inferred from it.

1 ☐ Most of the answers show fear.
2 ☐ Teenagers don't know what friendship is.
3 ☐ Adolescents don't know if romance or distance can complicate things.
4 ☐ Most of the teens are concerned about the importance of friendship.
5 ☐ Only huge actions are important among friends.

4 Read some of the answers from the teenagers in the text. Choose the one you like best. Then, explain why.

1 ☐ "Friends are kind of scary." Mary, 14.

2 ☐ "I have friends who I would confide anything in." Molly, 14.

3 ☐ "A true friend understands you, even when you're not talking." Casey, 14.

4 ☐ "I got sick, and my friend ran to the bathroom after me to hold my hair back as I became the Exorcist." Marissa, 16.

5 ☐ "Friends come and go." Lily, 14.

Extracted from: <http://kidshealth.org>. Accessed on: May 9, 2012.

Your explanation

___

___

___

Let's Talk about It

"As pessoas crescem e mudam", disse um dos adolescentes que responderam à pesquisa. Você concorda com isso? Acredita que, com o crescimento, as relações de amizade entre as pessoas mudam?

5 Practice the dialogues with a classmate. Use the cues given.

1

A: Had you cleaned your room when Mom arrived?

B: *Yes, I had.*

2

A: Had he washed the dishes when his wife phoned home?

B: *No, he hadn't.*

3

Had she prepared dinner when her children came back home?

4

Had he fixed the car when Jim arrived?

5

Had you done your homework when Julia called?

6

Had you finished lunch when Sue arrived?

7

Had he read the newspaper when Grandma arrived?

8

Had they left school when you saw them?

GRAMMAR

Past Perfect

O *Past Perfect* indica que uma ação ocorreu antes de outra ação no passado. É formado por *had* seguido do *particípio passado* do verbo principal.

I **had drunk** milk before I ate the bread.
'd

I **had drunk** milk.
You **had drunk** milk.
He **had drunk** milk.
She **had drunk** milk.
It **had drunk** milk.
We **had drunk** milk.
You **had drunk** milk.
They **had drunk** milk.

Interrogative: Had he **drunk** milk?

Negative: He **had not drunk** milk.
hadn't

Short answers:
Yes, he **had**. / No, he **hadn't**.

Questions
What had he **drunk** before he ate the bread?
Where had he **drunk** milk before he ate the bread?
Why had he **drunk** milk before he ate the bread?

6 Answer the questions. Give short answers. Use the cues in parentheses.

1 Had you done your homework before you watched TV? (Yes)

____

2 Had the teacher corrected the exercises before the bell rang? (Yes)

____

3 Had the guys played the guitar before the game started? (No)

____

4 Had you and your classmates finished the presentation when the director arrived? (Yes)

____

5 Had the girl started her speech when the lights went out? (No)

____

6 Had the children taken shower when you arrived? (Yes)

____

7 Complete the sentences with the Past Perfect of the verbs in parentheses.

1 She *had made* (make) a cake before I left.
2 Anne ______________ (see) the movie before she read the book.
3 Mr. Folks ______________ (build) that house before the kids were born.
4 The dog ______________ (eat) all the food when we arrived.
5 My parents ______________ (travel) for a month before they met their friends.

8 Fill in the blanks. Use the Simple Past or the Past Perfect.

1 We *had heard* (hear) about the accident when you *arrived* (arrive).
2 John and I ______________ (realize) that we ______________ (take) the wrong road.
3 She ______________ (say) that she ______________ (see) that show.
4 I ______________ (be) sure that he ______________ (give) the correct answer.
5 Dennis ______________ (correct) the homework which I ______________ (do).

GRAMMAR

Can (poder, conseguir) e *could* (pôde, podia, poderia) são sempre seguidos de verbo no infinitivo sem *to*:

He **can** speak three languages.
I **could** dance when I was young.
We **could** go home now.

9 Rewrite the sentences. Use *could.*

1 I can dance.
I could dance.

2 Can you help me?
____

3 Can I call you?
____

4 She can bring her friend.
____

5 You can do me a favor.
____

6 You can carry those boxes.
____

10 Listen to the sentences. Check the actions that happened first.

1 a

b

2 a

b

3 a

b

4 a

b

5 a

b

11 Think about your best friend. Then answer.

	yes	no	sometimes
Do you both like the same things?			
Do you both like the same music style?			
Do you tell each other your secrets?			
Do you trust in each other?			
Do you help each other?			
Do you listen to each other when you are sad?			
Are you happy when you are with him/her?			
Can you be yourself with your friend?			

Now count how many "yes" you have and check the score.

SCORE: 6 to 8 - You're really good friends.
5 to 7 - That's not bad, but you can improve your friendship!
Less than 5 - Better talk to your friend and check what's happening!

12 Read the answers of the teenagers on page 69 again. Then write about an episode in which you showed your friendship to someone or vice-versa.

FUN

13 Break the code. Find what people have said.

	1	2	3	4	5	6	7	8	9
A	am	cleans	drove	more	never	to	learned	just	is
B	yesterday	like	I	had	kitchen	a	Africa	seen	study
C	travel	giraffe	studies	has	beach	make	now	studying	on
D	English	likes	his	Sure!	the	cake	my	bought	friend
E	tomorrow	learn	made	have	car	ski	painted	we	this
F	teacher	swim	tickets	talk	been	you	mountains	makes	year
G	our	was	He	sleep	did	much	not	are	does
H	safari	going	every day	were	garage	South	Australia	agency	and

MOM

B3	E4	A8	F5	A6	B6	C1	H8.

B3	E4	D8	G1	F3	A6	H6	B7.

BOY

B3	E4	A5	B8	B6	C2.

GIRL

G8	E8	H2	C9	B6	H1?

MOM

D4!

25 **Key Language**

accompany	do	have	show
change	expect	say	talk
come	feel	see	tell
count	grow	seem	think

Way to Go

1 Complete the sentences. Use *can* or *could*.

1 Where's Chris? I ________________ not find her.

2 She ________________ help you with your homework, if you want.

3 He ________________ not swim when he was 4.

4 You ________________ leave now. It's not raining anymore.

2 Number the actions according to the order they happened.

1 When I got home, my little sister was scared. She had seen a cockroach.

a [*2*] I got home.

b [*1*] My little sister saw a cockroach.

2 When I got up, Dad had already left for work.

a [ ] I got up.

b [ ] Dad left for work.

3 He had finished his homework before he went to the sports club.

a [ ] He finished his homework.

b [ ] He went to the sports club.

4 The audience had started shouting before the band started singing.

a [ ] The audience started shouting.

b [ ] The band started singing.

5 When Grandma decided to bake a cake, aunt Anna had already arrived home.

a [ ] Grandma decided to bake a cake.

b [ ] Aunt Anna arrived home.

3 Write sentences about the following people's actions. Use *when* and the Past Perfect.

1 Edward had breakfast. Then he washed the dishes.
Edward had had breakfast when he washed the dishes.

2 Juliet had a shower. Then she called her friend.

____

3 Lucy arrived at the station. Then the train arrived there.

____

4 James read the book. Then he lent it to his classmate.

____

4 Read the following text and find:

1 The acronym for the United Nations ____________________

2 A word that indicates groups of people of the same nation ____________________

3 A word that corresponds to "conversation" ____________________

The International Day of Friendship

The International Day of Friendship was proclaimed in 2011 by the UN General Assembly with the idea that friendship between peoples, countries, cultures and individuals can inspire peace efforts and build bridges between communities.

The resolution [...] places particular emphasis on involving young people, as future leaders, in community activities that include different cultures and promote international understanding and respect for diversity. [...]

To mark the International Day of Friendship, the UN encourages governments, international organizations and civil society groups to hold events, activities and initiatives that contribute to the efforts of the international community towards promoting a dialogue among civilizations, solidarity, mutual understanding and reconciliation.

Extracted from: <www.un.org>. Accessed on: May 14, 2012.

5 Read the sentences below. Write F (fact) or O (opinion).

1 [ ] The celebration of the International Day of Friendship aims at bringing peace to peoples and countries.

2 [ ] Everybody loves to celebrate the date.

3 [ ] The International Day of Friendship becomes more fun if it's celebrated with young people.

4 [ ] The international community has actions in the name of peace.

8 The Sound of Music

1 Answer the questions.

1 Are you affected by music?

2 What about animals and plants? Can music affect them?

26 **2** Read the article about the effect of music on plants, animals, and human beings.

CULTURE

Plants and Music

Some scientists state that music can have a powerful influence not only on people but also on animals and plants.

During the last decades several researchers have carried out intensive series of studies to demonstrate it. The Muzak Corporation, for example, has performed experiments to determine the effects of "background music" on factory workers. When music was played continuously, the employees became less productive. When music was played for some periods of time, many times a day, they were more productive; rather than when no music was played!

Dorothy Retallack of Denver, Colorado, performed several experiments to demonstrate the effects of music on plants. She varied the tone, number of hours a day, and kinds of music. She reported that when she played acid rock or rock music the plants turned away from the loudspeaker and, after some weeks, they died. When she played soft music, North Indian music or classical music, the plants turned towards the speaker and became more beautiful and alive.

The plants "liked" jazz, and showed no reaction to country and western music!

C 8

Based on: <www.dovesong.com>. Accessed on: May 14, 2012.

3 Check the correct meaning of the underlined words.

1 "When music was played continuously [...]"

a ☐ without stopping b ☐ stopping at intervals

2 "[...] the plants turned towards the speaker [...]"

a ☐ to the opposite direction of b ☐ in the direction of

3 "[...] music can have a powerful influence not only on people [...]"

a ☐ weak b ☐ strong

4 "[...] the plants [...] became more beautiful and alive."

a ☐ with life b ☐ with happiness

5 "Some scientists state that music [...]"

a ☐ the condition of a person b ☐ say

4 Write T (true) or F (false) according to the text.

1 ☐ Plants have an influence on music.

2 ☐ Retallack performed experiments with plants.

3 ☐ Factory workers were more productive when no music was played.

4 ☐ The plants "loved" country music.

5 ☐ The Muzak Corporation performed experiments with people.

5 Answer the questions according to the text.

1 When were the workers less productive?

___

2 What happened when the plants "listened" to rock music?

___

3 When were the plants more beautiful?

___

4 What have the researchers tried to demonstrate?

___

Let's Talk about It

Alguns alunos dizem que ouvir música enquanto estudam facilita a concentração. Você concorda? Qual é sua opinião a respeito disso?

GRAMMAR

Indefinites (Some, Any, No)

Some (algum(ns), alguma(s)) é usado em frases afirmativas ou em perguntas, quando se oferece algo.
There are **some** students in the classroom.
Do you need **some** help?

No (nenhum(a)) é usado em frases negativas, com o verbo na forma afirmativa:
There are **no** students in the classroom.

Any (algum(ns), alguma(s), nenhum(a)) é usado em frases interrogativas e negativas:
Are there **any** students in the classroom?
There aren't **any** students in the classroom.

Usa-se *any* em frases afirmativas, com o sentido de "qualquer":
We can buy **any** picture from this painter.

6 Complete the sentences with *some*, *any* or *no*.

1 Deborah didn't see *any* of her teachers at the game.
2 I have ________ classes tomorrow.
3 My parents are going to visit ________ of their relatives in Peru.
4 He is buying ________ ice cream now.
5 There aren't ________ Indian restaurants in that district.
6 Ask Meg to sing ________ Italian songs.
7 Is there ________ fruit here?
8 I can't take a taxi because I have ________ money.

7 Change the sentences into the required form.

1 Julian bought some books yesterday. (negative)
Julian didn't buy any books yesterday.
2 You didn't buy any postcards. (interrogative)
____
3 There is some milk in the fridge. (negative)
____
4 There are some boys in the school gym. (interrogative)
____
5 She drinks no coffee in the morning. (affirmative)
____

8 Look at the pictures. Then practice the dialogue with a classmate.

1 ketchup / eggs
A: *Is there any ketchup in the fridge?*
B: *Yes, there is some.*
A: *Are there any eggs?*
B: *Yes, there are some.*

2 ice cream / oranges

3 water / tomatoes

4 ketchup / grapes

9 Talk to a classmate. Use the cues given.

1 salad / chicken
A: *Is there any salad on the table?*
B: *No, there isn't any salad there.*
A: *You mean there is no salad today?*
B: *Yes, but there is some chicken.*

2 water / juice

3 salt / ketchup

4 dessert / fruit

GRAMMAR

Indefinites (Compounds)

Something / **Somebody** / **Somewhere** (algo / alguém / algum lugar)
There is **something** wrong.
I saw **somebody** waiting for you.
His shoes are **somewhere** in his bedroom.

Nothing / **Nobody** / **Nowhere** (nada / ninguém / nenhum lugar)
She has **nothing** to do.
Nobody understands Japanese in my class.
Paul is **nowhere** in the house.

Anything / **Anybody** / **Anywhere** (algo; nada / alguém; ninguém / algum lugar; nenhum lugar)
There isn't **anything** to drink.
Is there **anybody** home?
The dog can be **anywhere**.

Everything / **Everybody** / **Everywhere** (tudo / todos / todo lugar)
Everything is perfect now.
Everybody here loves you.
I've looked for my purse **everywhere**.

Observação: quando usados como sujeito de orações, os *compounds* são seguidos por verbos na terceira pessoa do singular.

10 Check the alternative that best completes the sentences.

1 ________________ is dancing now.
a ☐ Everything b ☐ Everybody c ☐ Everywhere

2 There are books ________________ in this library.
a ☐ everything b ☐ everybody c ☐ everywhere

3 I'll give this book to ________________ here.
a ☐ something b ☐ somebody c ☐ somewhere

4 I can't find my new CD ________________.
a ☐ anything b ☐ anybody c ☐ anywhere

5 ________________ has a good reason to stay in bed on Sunday mornings.
a ☐ Everything b ☐ Everybody c ☐ Everywhere

6 ________________ is so beautiful like this place.
a ☐ Nothing b ☐ Nobody c ☐ Nowhere

7 Do you want ________________ to eat?
a ☐ anything b ☐ anybody c ☐ anywhere

11 Look at the pictures. Then practice the conversation with a classmate.

1

Joe / do

A: *What's the matter with Joe?*
B: *He has nothing to do.*
A: *What a pity!*

2

Beni / drink

3

Sandra / wear

4

The kids / do

5

You / read

27 **12** Listen to Mandy. Then check the correct answers to the following questions.

1 Where did everybody go last weekend?
a ☐ To the movies. b ☐ To the park.

2 How was it?
a ☐ It was boring. b ☐ It was fantastic.

3 What happened yesterday?
a ☐ Somebody decided to have a costume party. b ☐ Somebody decided to have a barbecue party.

4 Does Mandy like barbecues?
a ☐ Yes, she does. b ☐ No, she doesn't.

5 Did Mandy participate in the barbecue?
a ☐ Yes, she did. b ☐ No, she didn't.

6 What's Mandy's conclusion?
a ☐ Everywhere is a nice place if there are friends around. b ☐ Everywhere is a nice place when there is a barbecue.

13 Look at the painting *Meninos soltando pipas*, by Candido Portinari. Then check the sentences that describe it.

1 [ ] There are some boys.
2 [ ] There are no girls.
3 [ ] The kids are sad.
4 [ ] Some kites are red.
5 [ ] There are no boys wearing white.
6 [ ] There are no yellow kites.

14 Write eight sentences to describe the painting *Futebol* by Candido Portinari.

____

____

____

____

____

____

____

____

FUN

15 Find the hidden message.

P	L	A	N	T	S	O	H	Z	X
Y	E	E	K	C	H	I	U	L	A
M	E	M	V	E	Y	B	M	C	O
C	A	N	N	F	I	Z	A	T	M
L	O	V	I	F	T	O	N	B	U
B	I	C	O	A	S	E	T	E	S
A	L	A	B	Y	W	Z	T	P	I
K	A	N	I	M	A	L	S	R	C
S	S	T	Q	C	E	D	E	I	N

Sometimes, _ _ _ _ _   _ _ _   _ _ _ _ _ _

_ _ _ _ _ _, _ _ _ _ _ _ _

and _ _ _ _ _ beings.

Key Language

affect	carry out	human being	tone
alive	continuously	loudspeaker	towards
background	die	powerful	turn away
barbecue	factory	state	western

Way to Go

1 Answer the questions. Use the words given.

1 Are there any plants in your house? (some)

____

2 Will she need any eggs for that recipe? (any)

____

3 Do you have any Art Books about Portinari in your house? (no)

____

4 Did they watch any movies on TV yesterday? (any)

____

2 Rewrite the sentences. Correct them according to the pictures.

1 The dog hasn't seen anybody behind the gate.

The dog has seen somebody behind the gate.

2 There's something to eat in Jeff's house.

____

3 Anna has somewhere to go tonight.

____

4 There isn't anything strange in the X-ray.

____

5 They found nowhere to have dinner.

____

6 There's somebody wearing a yellow T-shirt.

____

3 Listen to the text. Number the following paragraphs according to what you hear.

Address: www.takingcharge.csh.umn.edu

Find

What is Music Therapy?

( ) [...] Sessions of music therapy are designed with a number of factors in mind, including the clients' physical health, communication abilities, cognitive skills, emotional well-being, and interests. [...]

( ) [...] Music therapy is the use of music to address the physical, emotional, cognitive, and social needs of a group or individual. It employs a variety of activities, such as listening to melodies, playing an instrument, drumming, and writing songs. Music therapy is appropriate for people of all ages. [...]

( ) [...] It touches all aspects of the mind, body, brain and behavior. Music can provide a distraction for the mind, it can slow the rhythms of the body, and it can alter our mood, which in turn can influence behavior. [...]

Extracted from: <www.takingcharge.csh.umn.edu>. Accessed on: August 2, 2012.

4 Match the words to their meaning, according to the text.

1 address
2 employs
3 slow
4 alter

a ( ) uses
b ( ) change
c ( ) reduce
d ( ) handle

5 Check the picture that best represents the profession mentioned in the text.

1

2
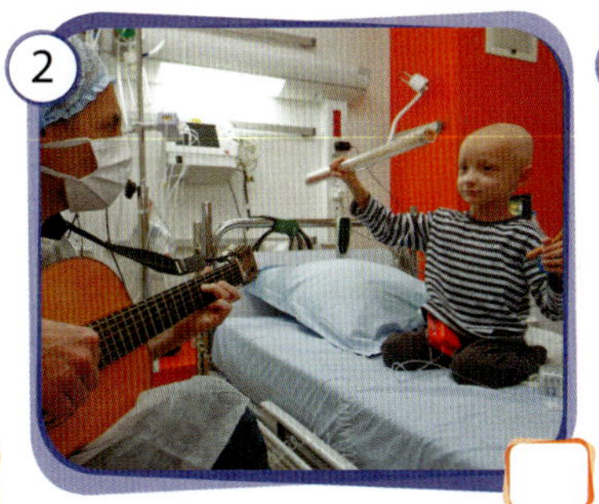

3

Extra Reading 1

A Brief History of Technology

500 b.C.

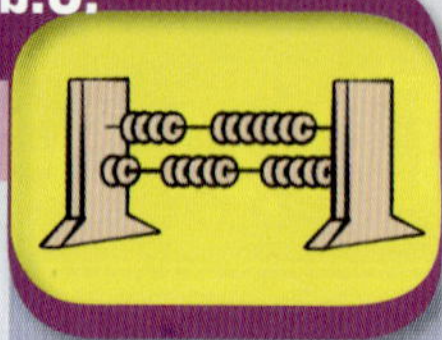

The Abacus calculator.

1821

First computer is created.

1939

Electric computer is created for routine use.

1971

First e-mail is sent.

1973

First computer with keyboard, mouse and graphical interface appears.

1975

First affordable home computer is launched.

1983

Global internet is created.

1994

Website navigations begin.

1998

Google Technology, Inc. is created.

2001

Wikipedia is online.

2004

Orkut is launched.

2005

YouTube is available.

2006

Facebook and Twitter are available.

2011

630 million estimated new users in Facebook.

Interesting Facts about the Internet

- Every day people send about 247 billion e-mails worldwide.
- Every week adolescents spend about 31 hours online, but they spend only 4 hours doing their homework.
- There are about 234 million websites available on the internet.
- 50 million tweets are sent every day. In 2009, 2.5 million tweets were sent per day.
- About 71% of users buy products online.

The Top Five Countries to Use Blogs Are:

1 The U.S.: 29.22%
2 United Kingdom: 6.75%
3 Japan: 4.88%
4 Brazil: 4.19%
5 Canada: 3.93%

Based on: <www.clemson.edu>; <www.joesblogg.com>. Accessed on May 15, 2012.

1 Based on the texts, match the columns.

1 People started using e-mail
2 The internet as we know it today
3 The first computer appeared
4 Teenagers of the digital age
5 More than 200 billion e-mails
6 2.5 million tweets were sent per day

a ☐ are sent every day.
b ☐ in 2009.
c ☐ was created in 1983.
d ☐ in 1821.
e ☐ only in 1971.
f ☐ spend long hours online and not so many hours doing their homework.

2 Read the definitions below. Find the corresponding words in the box.

adolescent	blog	calculator	internet	keyboard

1 A device for performing mathematical calculations, especially an electronic device that can be held in the hand. ________________

2 A shared online journal where people can post diary entries about their personal experiences and hobbies. ________________

3 A complete set of keys, usually hand-operated, as on a piano, organ, typewriter, or typesetting machine. ________________

4 A young person who has undergone puberty but who has not reached full maturity. ________________

5 An interconnected system of networks that connects computers around the world via the TCP/IP protocol. ________________

Extracted from: <www.thefreedictionary.com>. Accessed on: May 15, 2012.

PROJECT

Technology Quiz

- Work in pairs.
- Create a set of five questions about the history of technology.
- Use the information on the text on page 88 or do some research on the internet.
- Give each question a correct answer and three incorrect ones.
- With another pair of classmates, play the quiz and score points.

Extra Reading 2

The Rich Culture of BRAZIL

Brazilians Are the Most Diverse People around the World

European, Asian and Arab immigrants, African slaves and native Indians make the Brazilian culture a very rich and diverse one. Because of such blending of races, Brazilians can be considered the most ethnically diverse people in the world. Brazil is a huge country, and anywhere you travel to, this rich diversity is apparent on people's faces. Mainly if you are visiting large cities, you can see this exotic representation of different skin color, hair type, color of the eyes, and other physical traits.

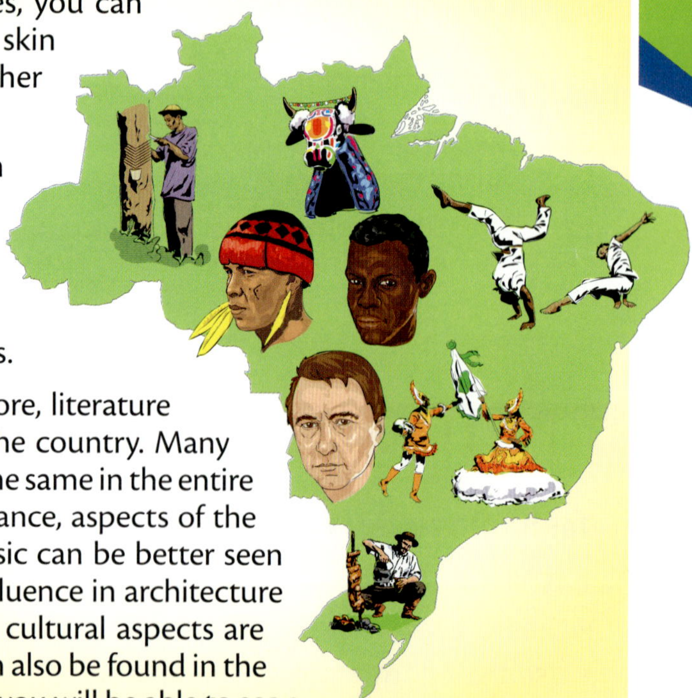

Brazil's history involves a Dutch invasion and a fight with Spain, but the Portuguese colonizers fought for their largest and richest colony. Consequently, our official language is Portuguese, and we are a unique people with cultural individualities.

In general, Brazil's architecture, art, folklore, literature and music exhibit the diverse culture of the country. Many aspects of this rich and diverse culture are the same in the entire country, while others are regional. For instance, aspects of the African influence in religion, food and music can be better seen in the northeast; European immigrants' influence in architecture is famous in the south; the native Indian's cultural aspects are visible in the north region; and all of this can also be found in the southeast. While traveling around in Brazil, you will be able to see a lot of its cultural features and differences, no matter what part of the country you are visiting.

Based on: <www.brazil-travelnet.com>. Accessed on: May 15, 2012.

1 Based on the text, check the correct alternative.

1 In the south region of the country:

a ☐ Indian cultural aspects are more common.

b ☐ European architecture is more evident.

2 Today, Brazil is a:

a ☐ rich and diverse country.

b ☐ Portuguese colony.

3 Brazil can be considered the most ethnically diverse country in the world:

a ☐ mainly because of its big size.

b ☐ mainly because of an evident blending of races.

2 Find the following information in the text.

1 Elements that represent aspects of the Brazilian culture

____

2 Evidence of African influence in the northeast region

____

3 Elements that make Brazilian culture rich and diverse

____

4 The region in Brazil where there is a mixture of all cultures

____

PROJECT

Brazil's Diversity Map

- Work in groups to create a diversity map of Brazil.
- Each group will work with each region of Brazil (north, south, southeast, northeast and central-west regions).
- Draw the map of the region you were assigned, only with the outlines.
- Look for pictures that represent the region. You can use the internet or go to a library. You can also draw if you can't find pictures.
- Illustrate your map with the pictures and drawings. There will be no texts, only images.
- Join your map with the maps of the other groups. Make a big Brazil's Diversity Map.
- Display it in the classroom.

Extra Reading 3

WOMEN WHO RULE THE WORLD

What Do Dilma Rousseff, Hillary Clinton and Sheikh Hasina have in common?

Besides being women, they have power. They rule the world because they are respected leaders who take important decisions and influence politics around the world.

Dilma Rousseff

In 2010, Dilma Rousseff was elected Brazil's first female president. She started her political career fighting against the dictatorship in the late 60's. She has also been the municipal secretary of finance in Porto Alegre, president of the state Economical and Statistical Foundation (FEE), Brazil's Secretary of Energy and Minister of Mines and Energy during a former administration.

Originally from Minas Gerais, the president has studied Economics at the Federal University of Rio Grande do Sul. Her main goal as president of Brazil is to fight against poverty.

Hillary Clinton

President Barack Obama appointed her and she accepted the second most powerful position in his administration. She became the U.S. Secretary of State. Hillary Clinton has already managed to restore diplomatic bonds with many nations that were politically distant from the U.S. during Bush's administration.

The former first lady, wife of the former U.S. President Bill Clinton, is admired and seen as a formidable female politician by many people.

Sheikh Hasina

The Prime Minister of Bangladesh, Sheikh Hasina, faces a great challenge in her position. She rules a nation that is extremely poor and politically unstable due to a great deal of corruption and hostile opposition. She has been trying to fight the high levels of unemployment and corruption in her country since the 2000's.

She has a firm proposal to help her country, to fight corruption and restore relations with other neighboring countries.

Based on: <http://educacao.uol.com.br>; <www.rediff.com>. Accessed on: May 15, 2012.

1 Find in the texts six words that are similar to Portuguese.

____

____

____

2 Read the sentences and write the corresponding number in parentheses. Use the code below.

a Dilma Rousseff   b Hillary Clinton   c Sheikh Hasina

1 ( ) Her main goal is to fight against poverty.
2 ( ) One of her goals is to fight corruption.
3 ( ) She has the second most important position of a very powerful country.
4 ( ) She started her political career fighting against dictatorship.
5 ( ) She's already been the first lady of her country.
6 ( ) She's been Prime Minister of an Asian country.

3 Read the sentences below. Check the correct ones, according to the texts.

1 ( ) The three women have important political functions in the world.
2 ( ) The three women are Presidents of their countries.
3 ( ) Sheikh Hasina is responsible for a country which has lots of political problems and corruption.
4 ( ) Dilma Rousseff was Brazil's Secretary of Energy before becoming president.

PROJECT

Biographies of Powerful Women in Brazil and around the World

- Work in small groups.
- You will be assigned an important female leader on the political and economical scene in the world.
- Do some research on the internet or at a library about her life.
- Write a short biography of her.
- Illustrate the biography with pictures, maps, drawings, etc.
- Show the biography to your classmates and exhibit it in another area of the school, so other students and teachers can see it.

CAPOEIRA

An Artistic Institution in Brazil

Brazilian *Capoeira* origins are related to a ritualistic African martial arts dance. The Afro-Brazilian slaves developed it about 400 years ago as a form of self-defense used against their masters. Slave owners prohibited it and banished it from the *senzalas* (slave barracks) in the sugar cane plantations, but the slaves practiced it secretly, and later on it was developed into an acrobatic dance, as a disguise. The prohibition lasted up until the 1920s, but Mestre Bimba (Manuel dos Reis Machado) changed this in the 1930s. In 1932, he officially opened up his own academy (Academia-escola de Capoeira Regional), transforming *capoeira* into a form of artistic expression that is now an institution in the state of Bahia.

The stringed musical instrument used in *capoeira* is called a *berimbau*. It looks like a fishing rod and it was used to alert the fighters when their masters were approaching. Later on, it became incorporated into the dance to maintain the rhythm.

There are two *capoeira* schools: the traditional Capoeira de Angola, led by Mestre Pastinha, and the regional *Capoeira*, started by Mestre Bimba.

Capoeira combines a form of fighting, game and dance. It's usually practiced by two fighters at a time inside a circle of spectators and fighters who clap and sing.

Besides the *berimbau*, other musical instruments are used, such as: the tambourine, bell and drum, which provide melodic support.

Capoeira gains more followers every year, both in Brazil and worldwide.

Based on: <www.capoeiranyc.com>; <www.gulabmahal.com>. Accessed on: May 15, 2012.

1 Read the text again. Then answer the following questions.

1 What did the slaves originally use the *berimbau* for?

____

2 Nowadays, what are the *berimbau* and the other musical instruments used for?

____

2 Look at the mind map below. Underline the words that are related to *capoeira*.

PROJECT

Martial Arts Magazine

- Work in groups to create an article for a Martial Arts Magazine.
- You will be assigned a martial art.
- Do some research on the internet or at a library about the martial art.
- Create a magazine article about it.
- Illustrate your article with pictures.
- With the articles of the other groups, organize the magazine, which can follow the structure below:
  1. Cover
  2. Opening text
  3. Table of contents
  4. Articles

Grammar Reference

Unit 1

Simple Future

O *Simple Future* é formado com *will* + o verbo principal.

É usado para expressar previsões sobre o futuro e decisões tomadas no momento da fala. O *Simple Future* também é usado para oferecer ajuda a alguém ou fazer um pedido.

It **won't** rain today.
The phone is ringing. I **will** answer it.
Will you help me with those boxes?

Em sentenças afirmativas, o auxiliar *will* vem antes do verbo.

I think I **will go** to the beach later.

Em sentenças negativas, o auxiliar *will* também vem antes do verbo e é seguido de *not*.

Grandma **won't tell** me the secret of her banana pie.

Em sentenças interrogativas, o auxiliar *will* vem antes do sujeito. Nas respostas curtas, usa-se *will* e *won't*.

A: **Will** you pass the final tests?
B: Yes, I **will**. / No, I **won't**.

Observação

As formas contraídas são *'ll* e *won't*.

They**'ll** go to the beach next month.
She **won't** sing a love song.

Simple Future + Question Words

A: **What will** they have for breakfast on the weekend?
B: They will have toast and orange juice.

A: **When will** you visit your sick relatives?
B: I will visit them on Saturday afternoon.

A: **Where will** we travel to on our vacation?
B: We will travel to the beach.

A: **How will** he come to the restaurant?
B: He will take a bus.

1 Match the sentences to complete the ideas.

1 Mrs. Alter is very thirsty.
2 Peter is tired.
3 The children are hungry.
4 It's a sunny day.
5 Grandma and Grandpa can't hear you.

a ☐ I'll make them some sandwiches.
b ☐ She will drink some water.
c ☐ We'll go out for a walk.
d ☐ OK, I'll turn down the stereo.
e ☐ He will rest.

Verb Tenses

Present Continuous

O *Present Continuous* expressa ações que estão acontecendo no momento da fala. É formado pelo verbo *to be* no *Simple Present* + o verbo principal seguido de *ing*.

The teacher **is explaining** a new lesson now.

Past Continuous

O *Past Continuous* expressa ações que estavam acontecendo em determinado momento no passado. É formado pelo verbo *to be* no *Simple Past* + o verbo principal seguido de *ing*.

We **were studying** for our tests last night.

Going to

Going to expressa ação planejada da decisão tomada. É formado pelo verbo *to be* no *Simple Present* + *going to* + o verbo principal.

Melissa **is going to come** for Christmas this year.

Simple Present

O *Simple Present* expressa ações habituais, de rotina, fatos ou verdades universais. É formado pelo:

- verbo no infinitivo sem *to* quando o sujeito for *I*, *you*, *we* ou *they*.

They walk in the park every Saturday.

- verbo no infinitivo sem *to* acrescido de *s*, *es* ou *ies* quando o sujeito for *he*, *she* ou *it*.

He usually **drinks** milk for breakfast

Nas formas interrogativa e negativa, usam-se os auxiliares *do* e *does*, acompanhando os verbos principais no infinitivo sem *to*.

She **doesn't talk** to people she doesn't know.
Do you **like** to go to the movies?

Simple Past

O *Simple Past* expressa ações que foram concluídas em um tempo definido no passado.

Para os verbos regulares, é constituído pela forma básica do verbo acrescida de *ed*, *d* ou *ied*. Para os verbos irregulares, usa-se a forma específica do verbo.

You **talked** on the phone for two hours last night.

We **went** to the mall yesterday morning.

Nas formas interrogativa e negativa, usa-se o auxiliar *did* acompanhando o verbo principal no infinitivo sem *to*.

I **didn't call** my best friend yesterday.

They **didn't have** classes last Friday.

Did you **visit** your grandparents last week?

Did she **buy** any souvenirs on her last trip to the U.S.?

Simple Future

O *Simple Future* expressa previsões, promessas e decisões tomadas no momento da fala. É formado por *will* + o verbo principal.

The test was easy. I think I'**ll get** a good grade!

2 Choose the right alternative. Then complete the sentences.

1 ______ you ______ the dentist next week?
a ☐ Do; see b ☐ Are; going to see

2 She always ______ her homework.
a ☐ was doing b ☐ does

3 The students ______ on the board when the teacher came in.
a ☐ were writing b ☐ are going to write

4 I ______ the movie on TV last night. It was too late!
a ☐ won't watch b ☐ didn't watch

5 He ______ on a report at the moment.
a ☐ was working b ☐ is working

Unit 2

Genitive Case (Review)

O *Genitive Case* (ou *Possessive Case*) é formado acrescentando-se um apóstrofo (*'*) ou um apóstrofo seguido de *s* (*'s*) após um substantivo para indicar o possuidor de algo.

Usa-se *'s* após substantivos não terminados em *s*.

That is my brother**'s** girlfriend.

Sandro**'s** shoes are dirty.

Usa-se apenas *'* após substantivos terminados em *s*.

The students**'** books are on the shelves.

My sisters**'** dresses are similar.

Sobre a quantidade de possuidores, temos:

- Quando há mais de um possuidor e um único objeto possuído, apenas o último possuidor recebe *'s* ou apenas *'*.

  Mrs. Almeida is Laura and João**'s** mother.

- Quando há mais de um possuidor para objetos diferentes, usamos *'s* ou apenas *'* após cada possuidor.

  Claudia**'s** and Eliane**'s** husbands are soccer fans.

Question Word Whose

Usa-se *Whose* para perguntar quem é o possuidor de determinada coisa.

whose?: de quem?

Whose cell phone is that?

It's Ligia**'s**.

1 Underline the correct alternative.

1 Ted borrowed my **husband'** / **husband's** scientific calculator.

2 The **women's** / **women'** restroom is on the left.

3 Mr. Taylor is **Cynthia's** / **Cynthia** English teacher.

4 Those are the **girls's** / **girls'** uniforms.

Possessive Adjectives and Pronouns

Os *Possessive Adjectives* são posicionados antes dos substantivos.

That is **my** bedroom.
What's **your** address?

Os *Possessive Pronouns* substituem os substantivos aos quais se referem.

Tania liked her new dress but her sisters didn't like **theirs** (= their dresses).

Possessive Adjectives	Possessive Pronouns
My	Mine
Your	Yours
His	His
Her	Hers
Its	Its
Our	Ours
Your	Yours
Their	Theirs

Os *Possessive Pronouns* podem ser usados depois de *of*:

This book is one **of hers**.
They are friends **of mine**.

2 Choose the correct alternative. Then complete the sentences.

1 Camilla and Thomas have pets. __________ is a cat and __________ is a dog.

a ☐ Hers; his b ☐ Her; his

2 Alicia and Robert are going to call __________ parents tonight. Are you going to call __________, too?

a ☐ their; yours b ☐ theirs; your

3 Send me __________ picture and I'll send you __________.

a ☐ yours; my b ☐ your; mine

4 Mr. Brown is __________ favorite teacher. But we can't decide who's __________.

a ☐ hers; our b ☐ her; ours

Unit 3

Should

Should expressa conselhos ou recomendações. Significa "deveria" ou "deve".

- Em sentenças afirmativas, usa-se *should* + o verbo principal:

  You'll be late for work. You **should take** a taxi.

- Em sentenças negativas, usa-se *shouldn't* (*should not*) + o verbo principal no infinitivo:

  It's really cold today. We **shouldn't go** to the beach.

- Em sentenças interrogativas, *should* vem antes do sujeito.

  A: He has a fever. **Should** he **go** to school tomorrow?

  B: Yes, he **should**. / No, he **shouldn't**.

1 Write sentences with the expressions from the box. Use *should* or *shouldn't*.

behave well
cheat in exams
concentrate on our studies
forget to do our homework
study at home every day
talk in class

To be good students,... *we should behave well.*

____

____

____

____

____

Reflexive Pronouns

Os *Reflexive Pronouns* são formados com as terminações *self* e *selves*.

Personal Pronouns	Reflexive pronouns
I	myself
You	yourself
He	himself
She	herself
It	itself
We	ourselves
You	yourselves
They	themselves

Usam-se os *Reflexive Pronouns* para indicar que o sujeito faz e sofre a ação do verbo. Eles concordam com o sujeito.

We should behave **ourselves** during classes.

Quando o *Reflexive Pronoun* é precedido por *by*, significa que a ação foi feita sem ajuda.

I can't carry this box **by myself**.

2 Unscramble the words to form sentences.

1 by / can't / The / eat / girl / baby / herself / .

____

2 Dad / shaving / didn't / cut / was / himself / he / while / .

____

3 yourself / Did / enjoy / party / the / at / you / yesterday / ?

____

4 myself / I / talk to / Sometimes / .

____

Unit 4

Present Perfect

O *Present Perfect* é usado para descrever ações que aconteceram em um tempo indeterminado no passado ou que se iniciaram no passado e não sabemos se ainda estão acontecendo no presente. É formado por *have/has* + o *Past Participle* do verbo principal.

O *Past Participle* dos verbos regulares tem a mesma forma que o *Simple Past*. Já no caso dos verbos irregulares, não há nenhuma regra a ser seguida. Consulte a lista de verbos irregulares na página 134.

I **have watched** many good films.
He **hasn't studied** much at home.

A: **Have** they **been** sick?
B: Yes, they **have**. / No, they **haven't**.

Observações

As formas contraídas são:

've = have **'s** = has
haven't = have not **hasn't** = has not.

Affirmative	Negative	Interrogative
I **have worked** hard.	I **haven't worked** hard.	**Have** I **worked** hard?
You **have slept** a lot.	You **haven't slept** a lot.	**Have** you **slept** a lot?
He **has danced** the mambo.	He **hasn't danced** the mambo.	**Has** he **danced** the mambo?
She **has cooked** lunch.	She **hasn't cooked** lunch.	**Has** she **cooked** lunch?
It **has been** sunny.	It **hasn't been** sunny.	**Has** it **been** sunny?
We **have done** the dishes.	We **haven't done** the dishes.	**Have** we **done** the dishes?
You **have played** chess.	You **haven't played** chess.	**Have** you **played** chess?
They **have listened** to music.	They **haven't listened** to music.	**Have** they **listened** to music?

1 Use the cues to write sentences in the Present Perfect.

1 your teacher / be / to France / ?
Has your teacher been to France?

2 I / see / a lot of soccer matches / .
____

3 Scott / not study / German / .
____

4 you / clean / your bedroom / ?
____

5 they / not do / the laundry / .
____

Present Perfect *versus* Simple Past

O *Present Perfect* é usado para indicar uma ação ocorrida em tempo passado não definido ou uma ação que começou no passado e continua no presente.

Judy **has traveled** abroad.
I **haven't met** my boyfriend.
Have the managers **called** you?

O *Simple Past* é usado para indicar uma ação que ocorreu em um tempo definido no passado.

Judy **traveled** abroad **in 2009**.
I **didn't meet** my boyfriend **last weekend**.
Did the managers **call** you **yesterday**?

2. Fill in the blanks with the verbs in the box. Use the Present Perfect or the Simple Past.

break
go
take (neg.)
wash

1 Jane ______________ her leg.
2 ______________ you ______________ the floor last Tuesday?
3 I ______________ the dog for a walk.
4 We ______________ to school on foot last week.

Unit 5

Present Perfect and Adverbs (Part I)

O *Present Perfect* pode ser usado com alguns advérbios:

- *Since*: para indicar o início de uma ação; significa "desde".

  I have studied English **since** 2005.
- *For*: para indicar a duração de um período específico; significa "por".

  She has been married **for** 10 years.
- *Ever*: para perguntas; significa "alguma vez".

  Have you **ever** traveled to Cancun?
- *Never*: para sentenças afirmativas com sentido negativo; significa "nunca".

  They have **never** come to my place.

Present Perfect and Adverbs (Part II)

O *Present Perfect* também pode ser usado com:

- *Just*: para indicar uma ação que acabou de acontecer; significa "há pouco tempo".

  He has **just** left the office.
- *Already*: para sentenças afirmativas e interrogativas; significa "já".

  The dog has **already** eaten its food.
- *Yet*: para sentenças negativas e interrogativas; significa "ainda não" ou "já".

  I haven't finished my homework **yet**.
  Have you cleaned your room **yet**?
- *Lately*: indica ações que têm acontecido nos últimos tempos; significa "ultimamente".

  I have met your sister on my way to work **lately**.

1. Complete the dialogues with the correct Adverb.

1 **A:** Has she ______________ lived in an apartment?
B: No, she has ______________ lived in an apartment. She prefers houses.

2 **A:** Have you seen any good plays ______________?
B: Nope! I have worked hard ______________ the past month and I haven't had time.

3 **A:** Have you heard from Peter and Gabriela ______________?
B: No. In fact, I haven't met them ______________. What's up?
A: They have ______________ broken up.
B: Oh, really? And how are they doing?
A: Gabriela has ______________ moved on and decided to get down to her studies but Peter has ______________ felt so lonely!

4 **A:** Carlos hasn't been to the office ______________ May.
B: Yeah, I heard he has come down with a terrible cold.

Unit 6

Relative Pronouns: Who (That) / Where

Os *Relative Pronouns* referem-se a termos mencionados anteriormente e são usados para introduzir uma nova oração à oração principal.

Who (quem, que, o/a qual , os/as quais) é usado quando o antecedente é uma pessoa. Pode ser substituído por *that*.

The boy asked your name. He is my cousin.

The boy **who** (**that**) asked your name is my cousin.

Where (onde, em que, no/a qual, nos/as quais) é usado quando o antecedente é um lugar.

The store is next to the post office. I buy my clothes there.

The store **where** I buy my clothes is next to the post office.

Relative Pronouns: Which / Whose

Which (que, o/a qual, os/as quais) é usado quando o antecedente são coisas ou animais. Ele pode ser substituído por *that*.

The animal is under your bed. It's your dog.

The animal **which** (**that**) is under your bed is your dog.

Whose (cujo(s), cuja(s)) é usado para indicar posse.

Mary is a swimmer. Her scores were the best ones in our last competition.

Mary is a swimmer **whose** scores were the best ones in our last competition.

1 Unscramble the words to form sentences.

1 where / town / is / born / The / small / old / 320 / years / I / was / .

____

2 Andrea / with / work / is / children / the / to / teacher / prefers / who / .

____

3 orange / boy / whose / cap / The / tennis / is / is / player / a / .

____

4 wearing / she / beautiful / clothes / is / are / which / The .

____

Unit 7

Past Perfect

O *Past Perfect* é usado para indicar ações que aconteceram antes de outras ações no passado. É formado por *had* + o *Past Participle* do verbo principal.

When the police arrived, the thieves **had escaped**.

Clarisse **hadn't called** me before I got home.

A: **Had** the girls **made** their beds before they had lunch?

B: Yes, they **had**. / No, they **hadn't**.

Observações

As formas contraídas são:

'd = had

hadn't = had not

1 Complete the sentences with the verbs from the box. Use the Past Perfect.

be
brush
have
leave
score

1 Before the bell rang all the students ______________ in their classrooms.

2 When my mother told me to go to bed, I ______________ already ______________ my teeth.

3 By the time the basketball game finished, the girls ______________ 72 points.

4 After he ______________ a car accident, he started to drive more carefully.

5 ______________ the school bus ______________ when you got to the bus stop?

Can, Could

Can (pode, consegue) e *could* (pôde, podia, poderia) são usados para expressar capacidade e habilidade.

He **can** read without his glasses now but he **couldn't** before the operation.

Can e *could* são seguidos de verbos no infinitivo sem *to*:

He **can swim** as fast as a professional swimmer.

He **could take part** in marathons 10 years ago.

Can e *could* não precisam de auxiliares; na forma interrogativa, são colocados antes do sujeito; na forma negativa, usa-se *cannot* (*can't*) ou *could not* (*couldn't*):

A: **Can** you drive, Susan?

B: Sure! I **couldn't** drive when I was younger but nowadays I **can** drive very well.

2 Match the columns to form meaningful sentences.

1 Sarah can speak
2 My neighbors couldn't play
3 Can you dance
4 I can't write
5 Dawson could
6 Could we

a ( ) go out alone at night when we were 14 years old?
b ( ) four different languages.
c ( ) ride a bike to school last year.
d ( ) board games because they didn't know how to.
e ( ) in French, but I can read texts in that language.
f ( ) hip hop too or just the salsa?

Unit 8

Indefinites

Os *Indefinites some*, *any* e *no* são usados para indicar a existência ou não de alguma coisa.

- *Some* (algum(a), alguns(mas)) é usado em frases afirmativas. Também é usado em frases interrogativas, para oferecer algo a alguém.

  There are **some** DVDs I would like to buy.

  Would you like **some** help with dinner?

- *Any* (algum(a), alguns(mas), nenhum(a)) é usado em frases negativas ou interrogativas.

  There aren't **any** good hotels in my city.

  Are there **any** good movies on TV?

- *Any* pode ser usado em frases afirmativas com o significado de "qualquer".

  Grandchildren can't order **any** junk food when they are hanging out with their grandparents!

- *No* (nenhum(a)) é usado em frases negativas, com o verbo na forma afirmativa.

  There are **no** classes today. The teacher is sick.

  Poor Jarold! He has **no** friends.

1 Circle the correct alternative.

1 There aren't **no / any / some** new emails in my mailbox.

2 I bought **no / any / some** fresh fruit for dessert, but I want some.

3 Melina can't join us at the club because she has **no / any / some** math exercises to do.

4 **No / Any / Some** people spend their free time gossiping about their relatives.

Indefinite (Compounds)

Os *Compounds* seguem as mesmas regras do emprego de *some*, *any* e *no*.

- *Something / Somebody / Somewhere*: algo, alguém, algum lugar.

  There is **something** I can do to help you. I'm sure!

  I need to get in touch with **somebody** to take care of my baby tonight.

  I lost my folder **somewhere** in the studio.

- *Nothing / Nobody / Nowhere*: nada, ninguém, nenhum lugar.

  Nothing worries me today, it's my birthday!

  There was **nobody** I could talk to last night.

  I've looked all around and the children are **nowhere** in this mall.

- *Anything / Anybody / Anywhere*: algo ou nada, alguém ou ninguém, algum lugar ou nenhum lugar.

  Thank God I didn't have **anything** important in my bag when I was robbed!

  Was there **anybody** in the classroom when you arrived?

  Let's go **anywhere** you want tonight. It's up to you!

- *Everything / Everybody / Everywhere*: tudo, todos, todo lugar.

  I did **everything** the nurse told me to do.

  Everybody is waiting for the movie to start.

  Everywhere I go I think of you.

Quando usamos os *Compounds* como sujeito de oração, eles são seguidos por um verbo na terceira pessoa do singular:

Nobody treats me as well as you do.

Everything looks nice around here!

2 Complete the sentences with the appropriate Compound.

1 Clara is looking for her boyfriend but she can't find him ________________.

2 The teacher said there isn't ________________ wrong with my test.

3 ________________ has told me that Sylvio was fired. Is that true?

4 I studied for the finals by myself. ________________ helped me.

5 Let's go ________________ near the mountains on our next vacation, Janet?

6 I searched the internet for information on the doctor but I found ________________.

Workbook

Name:

Number: | Class: | Date:

1 Look at Bonnie's next week's planner. Then complete the sentences.

Sunday	Go to Brian's party at 8:00 p.m.
Monday	Go to the gym at 9:00 a.m.
Tuesday	See the dentist at 1:30 p.m.
Wednesday	Take Charlie to the vet at 3:00 p.m.
Thursday	Go to the gym at 9:00 a.m.
Friday	Get a new hair cut at 2:45 p.m.
Saturday	Go to the rock concert with Anna and Tommy at 7:00 p.m.

1 On Sunday *Bonnie will go to Brian's party* at 8:00 p.m.

2 She ______________________________ on Monday and Thursday at 9:00 a.m.

3 She _______________ take her dog Charlie to the vet on Wednesday at 5:00 p.m.

4 Bonnie _______________ have lunch on Tuesday at 1:30 p.m.

5 She ______________________________ on Friday at 2:45 p.m.

6 Anna and her friend Tommy ______________________________ with Bonnie at 7:00 p.m.

7 She _______________ go to the supermarket on Friday at 2:45 p.m.

2 Turn the negative sentences from exercise 1 into affirmative. Correct them according to Bonnie's planner.

1 ____

2 ____

3 ____

4 ____

5 ____

6 ____

7 ____

3 Complete the sentences with the correct verb tense of the verbs in the box. Use the cues given.

✓ = affirmative
✗ = negative

arrive	buy	do	go (3x)	have	study	walk (2x)

1 John ______________ English classes on Monday and Wednesday afternoons. (✓)

2 Jeremy ______________ a new shirt on Friday. He ______________ to the mall on Sunday. (✗ – ✓)

3 Akira ______________ to Japan three months ago. He ______________ to Korea (✗ – ✓)

4 Penny ______________ the laundry right now. (✓)

5 I ______________ my dog every day. Sometimes my sister ______________ him. (✗ – ✓)

6 Cindy ______________ Math at college next year. (✓)

7 We ______________ at Curitiba at 9:30 yesterday. (✓)

4 Read the article below. Then answer the questions.

Address: www.oway4.com

Find

Will the robot-maid be a dream come true?

By Helen Travis

Would you like to have a robot that is able to do all your tasks? How will housewives appreciate a robot that can set the table and wash the dishes?

We all wish for a robot that can do our work. It will be simply perfect when we have a robot to clean our houses, take care of the clothes, cook the meals and help us with school work. Certainly, we will have more time to read a book, watch TV, talk to family and hang out with friends.

Maybe in the future, engineers and scientists will develop sophisticated technology and create a robot very similar to humans and it will be able to help us. Do you think it is possible?

Engineers from Honda think so. They created the Asimo. Asimo can walk, run and climb stairs. It can also comprehend and respond to voice commands. Besides, it is similar to a human. It has arms, hands, legs and feet. Well, it seems that the future is really near.

1 Why do people wish for a robot-maid?

a ☐ Because it can be in charge of people's tasks at home.

b ☐ Because it will be people's friend.

2 What are Asimo's abilities?

a ☐ It can correspond to people's feelings for it.

b ☐ It can walk, run, climb stairs, comprehend and respond to voice commands.

3 How similar to human beings is Asimo?

a ☐ It has arms, hands, legs and feet.

b ☐ It has brain and heart.

Workbook

Name:

Number: Class: Date:

1 Circle the correct alternative.

1 Giulia is from Italy and **hers** / **her** husband is from Brazil.
2 My dad bought a car. **He** / **His** new car is big and red.
3 **My** / **Mine** new laptop is modern and fast. How about **your** / **yours**?
4 We have a beautiful white rabbit. **Its** / **It** name is Cotton Ball.
5 **Her** / **Hers** beach house is very big, but **my** / **mine** is small.
6 This English book is not **my** / **mine**. It's **your** / **yours**.

2 Complete the sentences with the correct Pronoun.

1 This is Jane's blue sweater. It's *hers*.
2 That soccer ball belongs to William. It's ______________.
3 The piano belongs to my uncle Jim and my aunt Melissa. It's ______________.
4 This delicious birthday cake is for me. It's ______________.
5 You have a beautiful kitten. It's ______________.

3 Answer the questions using Pronouns.

1 Whose laptop is this? (John)
It's his.
2 Is this Howard's new car? (Susan)
No it isn't. It's hers.
3 Are those my black pens? (Joanna and Stephanie)
____
4 Is this MP4 yours? (Thereza)
____
5 Whose DVDs are these? (Leonard and I)
____
6 Is this blue jacket yours? (Lucas)
____

4 Unscramble the words to form questions. Then use the information in parentheses to answer them.

1 garden / Whose / this / is / ?

Whose garden is this?

This is Mrs. Brown's garden. (Mrs. Brown)

2 that / Whose / is / car / new / ?

____

______________________________ (my grandfather)

3 Whose / is / magazine / it / ?

____

______________________________ (Alan)

4 hat / that / is / Whose / ?

____

______________________________ (my aunt Alicia)

5 they / are / shirts / Whose / ?

____

______________________________ (Mark)

5 Look at the pictures. Then ask questions and answer them. Use the cues given.

1

new tablet

Whose new tablet is it?

It's Ray's. (Ray)

2

kittens

Whose kittens are they?

They're mine. (my)

3

backpack

____

______________________________ (she)

4

guitar

____

______________________________ (he)

5

books

____

______________________________ (Sophie)

6

boots

____

______________________________ (Peter)

Workbook

Name:

Number: | Class: | Date:

1 Circle the Reflexive Pronouns. Then underline the words that they refer to.

1 The kids picked up all their toys by themselves yesterday.
2 Mrs. Miller's cat cleans itself every day in the morning.
3 Grandma made a chocolate cake to herself.
4 Tom and Nelson are going to hurt themselves if they play soccer on the wet floor.
5 Dr. Stevens decided to travel to India by himself next month.

2 Choose the correct alternative. Then complete the sentences.

1 We bought ________________ a new laptop because ours was too slow.
   a ☐ ourselves
   b ☐ themselves
2 Grandpa can't use the internet by ________________.
   a ☐ himself
   b ☐ herself
3 My dog hurt ________________ while running after a cat in the street.
   a ☐ myself
   b ☐ itself
4 I'll go to the mall by ________________ to buy a new pair of pants.
   a ☐ myself
   b ☐ ourselves
5 Brenda and Louise, I hope you enjoy ________________ at the theater tonight.
   a ☐ yourself
   b ☐ yourselves
6 Mom cut ________________ when she was chopping some tomatoes for the salad.
   a ☐ himself
   b ☐ herself

3 Give these people some advice. Use *should* or *shouldn't* and the cues given.

1 My hamster looks sick. (you / take it to the vet today)

You should take it to the vet today.

2 Mike is obese. (he / eat junk food every day)

____

3 Mary's son broke his leg playing soccer. (she / take him to the hospital)

____

4 Katherine doesn't like cats. (you / buy her a cat for her birthday)

____

5 You look sad. (you / come to Bob's party tonight)

____

4 Read Celine's wrote to an advice columnist, Aunt Sally. Then complete Aunt Sally's answer with *should* or *shouldn't* and the verbs in parentheses.

Aunt Sally – Columnist

Dear Aunt Sally,

My name is Celine. I'm 14 years old. I'm from Sydney, in Australia. I'm going on an exchange student program to Brazil. I'm going to stay in Rio de Janeiro with a nice family. I'm very excited. I heard they have beautiful beaches there, but I'm a little scared too. I don't know anybody in Brazil yet, but I'm eager to make lots of friends and I want to learn Portuguese. What should I do?

Thanks a lot.

Celine

Dear Celine,

You _______________ (get) worried about your exchange program. You _______________ (go) to Rio de Janeiro and you _______________ (make) new friends. I've heard Rio de Janeiro is a beautiful city. If that makes you feel better, you _______________ (learn) some Portuguese before you go. You _______________ (buy) a good English-Portuguese dictionary and you _______________ (teach) yourself about five new words a day. You _______________ (listen) to some Brazilian music to get used to what this language sounds like. Don't be scared at all. You will probably have a great experience and meet great friends soon.

Good luck and have fun!

Aunt Sally

Workbook

Name:

Number: | Class: | Date:

1 Complete the verb chart with the missing verb forms.

INFINITIVE	SIMPLE PAST	PAST PARTICIPLE
be	was / were	
drive		
eat	ate	
fly		flown
		gone
see		seen
sell		
		spoken
	talked	
		walked
write	wrote	

2 Choose four verbs from the list above. Write two sentences for each: one in the Simple Past and one in the Present Perfect.

1 *Where were you yesterday?*
Have you been to Los Angeles?

2 ______________________________

____

3 ______________________________

____

4 ______________________________

____

5 ______________________________

____

3 Match the columns to complete the sentences.

1 Ariano Suassuna ______________ *Auto da Compadecida* in 1955.
2 Grandpa ______________ to Korea last year.
3 I ______________ my paper some minutes ago.
4 I think Samantha ______________ her wallet.
5 That author ______________ many famous books.
6 My grandmother ______________ to Japan twice.
7 Sarah told me she ______________ her pencil case yesterday.
8 The students ______________ their tests.

a [ ] went
b [ ] has written
c [ ] wrote
d [ ] haven't finished
e [ ] finished
f [ ] has lost
g [ ] has been
h [ ] lost

4 Unscramble the words below to write sentences.

1 haven't / I / played / tennis / .

____

2 many / I / Brasília / been / to / times / have / .

____

3 himself / his / computer / Timothy / fixed / by / has / .

____

4 Spanish / Has / homework / Cynthia / finished / her / ?

____

5 Anna / dog / Benjamin and / found / their / Have / ?

____

5 Answer the questions. Use the options from the box.

an umbrella	because it's started raining	by train
Paul's daughter	to the supermarket	

1 What have you bought?

____

2 Where has he gone?

____

3 Why have the children come home?

____

4 How has she traveled?

____

5 Whose daughter have you seen?

____

Workbook

Name:

Number: Class: Date:

1 Complete the sentences with the words from the box. Use each word only once.

already	ever	for	just	never	since	yet

1 Bob and Theresa have lived in Quebec ______________ they were born.
2 Howard has ______________ had hamburger and French fries for dinner.
3 Have you and your family ______________ been to the mountains?
4 Michael has ______________ learned how to play the drums.
5 Mom has ______________ baked the chocolate cake for the party.
6 Sarah plays the piano very well. She has had piano lessons ______________ 12 years.
7 The train from Belo Horizonte hasn't arrived ______________.

2 Write sentences with the words below. Use the Present Perfect and the words in parentheses.

1 I / live / in Barcelona / 2001 (since)

____

2 Molly / see (neg.) / the newest Tom Cruise action movie (yet)

____

3 Paul / work / in that company / 12 years (for)

____

4 you / be / to London (ever)

____

5 Samuel / win / sports trophy (never)

____

6 Dad / arrive / from work (just)

____

7 She / travel / to the U.S. (already)

____

3 Read the dialogue between Linda and Sam. Complete it with the verbs given.

Address: www.owaychat.com | Find

O-Way chat

Linda: ____________ you ever ____________ (participate) in a chess tournament?

Sam: Yes, I ____________ (do) it in my old school.

Linda: Really! When ____________ it ____________ (happen)?

Sam: It ____________ (happen) two years ago.

Linda: Where ____________ (be) it?

Sam: It ____________ (be) in California, where I ____________ (live) before I ____________ (move) to Brazil.

Linda: Cool! ____________ you ____________ (win) first prize?

Sam: Yes, I have.

Linda: ____________ you ____________ (win) a trophy, Sam?

Sam: Yes, two trophies.

Linda: Good for you!

Sam: Yeah! It was a great experience.

Linda | Sam

4 Answer the questions based on Linda and Sam's dialogue above.

1 Has Sam ever participated in a chess tournament before?

____

2 When did Sam's chess tournament happen?

____

3 Where did the tournament happen?

____

4 How many trophies has Sam won?

____

5 Give true answers about yourself.

1 Have you ever gone camping with your friends?

____

2 Have you ever slept in a sleeping bag?

____

3 Have you ever participated in any tournament?

____

Workbook

Name:

Number: | Class: | Date:

1 Match the columns to form complete sentences.

1 A printer is a machine
2 This is the new cell phone
3 He's the man
4 Do you remember the car
5 That's the band
6 Old McCarthy's is the store
7 A key is an object

a ☐ which locks the door.
b ☐ whose song is on top in the hit parade.
c ☐ that I want to have.
d ☐ which prints documents.
e ☐ that your father liked?
f ☐ where you can find anything you want.
g ☐ who bought that house.

2 Join the sentences using *who*, *which*, *that*, *where* or *whose*.

1 

1 That is the boy. He broke the window.
That is the boy who broke the window. / That is the boy that broke the window.

2 

3 

4 

5 

2 Here is the travel information. We need to know it.

____

3 This is a big house. My grandma lives here.

____

4 That lady is my Science teacher. She is wearing a blue dress.

____

5 The woman talked to the mechanic. Her car is broken.

____

3 Read the text and underline the Relative Pronouns.

YOUR PET

Choose the Best Pet for Your Kids

For a child, to have a pet in the house where he/she lives is a great experience. It will help them to learn how to treat animals with love and respect, besides teaching them to have responsibility. This is good for the child to develop a caring attitude towards people, life and animals.

What pet to choose for a child who lives in a city?

A good option is to have small pets as rabbits, guinea pigs or mouses. They are cheap and easy to care for. A goldfish or an ant farm are good for parents who have a busy life. They're not expensive to care for. The ant farm is something which can help you teach your kids about organization skills and team work.

A hamster is a sweet pet whose sleeping habits are a little bit different: they sleep during the day and come out at night to play. For a child who likes to play with his/her pet, this is probably not a good option.

A puppy is a great companion for your child, but they cost a bit more to care for.

Parents will have to teach their kids to feed, groom, train, walk and play with the dog.

A cat is a cute animal. You don't need to walk it.

Choosing your pet carefully and responsibly will help your pet to become your kid's best friend. They can develop a loving bond which will not easily be broken.

23

Based on: <www.squidoo.com>. Accessed on: June 8, 2012.

4 Based on the text above, write T (true) or F (false).

1 ☐ Hamsters sleep at night and play during the day.
2 ☐ Children can learn how to treat animals with love and respect.
3 ☐ A rabbit, a guinea pig or a mouse are small pets.
4 ☐ A puppy is a great companion for your child.

Workbook

Name:

Number: | Class: | Date:

1 Read the sentences and circle the correct alternative.

1 Alicia **can't** / **couldn't** swim when she was three years old. She learned how to swim when she was six.
2 Grandma did not take any dance lessons when she was younger, but she **can** / **can't** dance very well.
3 It's raining cats and dogs! You **could** / **can't** go out.
4 Billy **couldn't** / **can't** get to school yesterday. He missed his school bus.
5 Where is my key chain? I **could** / **can't** find it anywhere.
6 These bags look very heavy, Mrs. Simmons. Wait, I **can** / **could** help you carry them.

Affirmative
Can
Could

Negative
Can't
Couldn't

2 Answer the questions. Use the expressions from the box.

a very good movie — have breakfast — Paris — their new roommate — yes

1 What had Amy done before she went to school?
She had had breakfast before she went to school.
2 Where had Paul and Alicia gone before they got married?
____
3 Had Alex already finished the report when his boss arrived?
____
4 Who had Monica and Carmen met before they moved in?
____
5 What had Charlie watched before he went to bed?
____

3 Make sentences with the cues given. Use *when*.

1 Your sister / clean her bedroom / your mother arrives home
Your sister had cleaned her bedroom when your mother arrived home.

2 Mathew / not wash the dishes / his wife calls him

____

3 Carol / prepare a special dinner / her parents come to visit her

____

4 Jeff's father / not repair the car / he goes to the soccer game

____

5 The cleaners / clean the office / Mr. Robertson arrives to work

____

4 Write sentences about the pictures. Use *can*, *can't*, *could* or *couldn't*.

1

2

1 I / speak English and Portuguese
I can speak English and Portuguese.

3

4

5

6

2 William / play tennis well when he was younger

____

3 Bernadette / speak Russian

____

4 Chris / play the electric guitar

____

5 Lindsay / bake a strawberry cake

____

6 Susan / swim when she was young

____

Workbook

Name:

Number: Class: Date:

1 Rewrite the sentences in the correct box. Complete them.

Can I borrow ____________ white flour to bake a cake?
I have ____________ idea how to get to the art museum from here.
Mom, is there ____________ coffee left?
My kids and I saw ____________ monkeys at the zoo yesterday.
Tom and Sally went to the movies without ____________ money.
We have ____________ money left to pay for hamburgers.

Some

Any

No

2 Check the correct sentences.

1 a ☐ There is anything stuck in my eye.
  b ☐ There is something stuck in my eye.

2 a ☐ Can anybody tell me what happened at the bank?
  b ☐ Can somewhere tell me what happened at the bank?

3 a ☐ This restaurant is crowded. Can we have dinner nowhere else tonight?
  b ☐ This restaurant is crowded. Can we have dinner somewhere else tonight?

4 a ☐ When I arrived home, everybody was there for the surprise party.
  b ☐ When I arrived home, anywhere was there for the surprise party.

5 a ☐ The children are something in the house.
  b ☐ The children are nowhere in the house.

3 Place the words from the box in the correct column.

something nobody anywhere somebody nowhere
anything somewhere nothing anybody

THINGS	PEOPLE	PLACES

4 Complete the dialogue between Amanda and David. Use *anything, nothing, something* or *somewhere*.

Address: www.ourchat.com

Find

OUR CHAT

Amanda: I have to write a school report about the Laws of Physics. Do you know ________________ about it, David?

David: No, I know ________________ about it. Sorry. Maybe, Stephanie knows ________________ about it. Give her a call.

Amanda: No, she doesn't know ________________. I've already talked to her.

David: Oh, I have an idea! Look at Dad's old encyclopedia. Maybe there is ________________ about it there.

Amanda: Brilliant. Where is it?

David: It's ________________ in his office.

Amanda: Thanks for your help. You're the best!

Amanda

David

Amanda Send

5 Read the dialogue above again. Write T (true) or F (false).

1 ☐ David is an expert in Laws of Physics.
2 ☐ Stephanie can help Amanda.
3 ☐ David thinks that their dad's old encyclopedia can help Amanda.
4 ☐ Their father is in the office, and they know where.

Glossary

A

a um(a)
a great deal uma grande quantidade
a little um pouco
a little bit um pouco
a lot muito
a lot of muitos(as)
Abacus ábaco
abandoned abandonado(a)
ability habilidade
able capaz
about cerca de, em torno de; sobre
above acima
abroad em outro país
academy academia, escola
accept aceitar
accepted aceito(a)
access acessar
accessed on acessado(a) em
accident acidente
accompany acompanhar
according to de acordo com
account conta (bancária)
acid rock *rock* psicodélico
acrobatic acrobático(a)
across horizontal (em uma palavra cruzada)
act agir; ato
action ação
active ativo(a)
activity atividade
actor ator
actually na verdade
adapted from adaptado(a) de
add acrescentar, adicionar
address direcionar, encaminhar; endereço
adjective adjetivo
administration administração
administrator administrador(a)
admired admirado(a)
adolescent adolescente
adult adulto(a)
adverb advérbio
advice conselho
affect afetar, influenciar
affected influenciado(a)
affirmative afirmativo(a)
affordable acessível
African africano(a)
Afro-Brazilian afro-brasileiro(a)
after após, depois de; atrás
afternoon tarde
again de novo, novamente
against contra
age era, idade
agency agência
ago atrás
air aéreo(a)
airplane avião
alert alertar
A-list de primeira linha, *top*
alive vivo(a), vívido(a)
all todos(as); tudo
all over the world no mundo todo
all right tudo bem
all through the year o ano todo
almost quase
alone sozinho(a)
alongside ao lado de
alphabet alfabeto
already já
also também
alter alterar
alternative alternativo(a); alternativa (opção)
always sempre
amazing incrível
among entre (duas ou mais pessoas ou coisas)
an um, uma
anarchy anarquia
and e
animal animal
another outro(a)
answer responder; resposta
ant farm criação de formiga
any algum(a); nenhum(a); qualquer
anybody alguém; ninguém
anything algo, alguma coisa; nada
anywhere algum lugar; nenhum lugar
apartment apartamento
apparent aparente, visível
appear aparecer, surgir
appearance aparência
appreciate apreciar, prezar
appoint apontar
approach aproximar
appropriate adequado(a), apropriado(a)
April abril
Arab árabe
architecture arquitetura
area área
arm braço
army exército
around ao redor; por aí; por volta de
arrive chegar
art arte
article artigo
artist artista
artistic artístico(a)
as à medida que; como; uma vez que
as much... as tanto... quanto
asap (as soon as possible) o quanto antes; o mais rápido possível
Asian asiático(a)
ask pedir; perguntar
aspect aspecto
assign atribuir
asteroid asteroide
astonished maravilhado(a)
at às; em, no(a)
atomic bomb bomba atômica
atomic bombing ataque com bomba atômica
attached anexo(a)
attitude postura
August agosto
aunt tia
author autor(a)
available disponível
award prêmio

B

baby bebê
background music música de fundo
backpack mochila
backyard jardim
bad ruim
bag bolsa
bake assar
ball bola
banana banana
band banda
banish banir, expulsar
bank banco (instituição financeira)
bar barra
barbecue churrasco
based on baseado(a) em; com base em
basketball basquetebol
bathroom banheiro
battery bateria
battle batalha
be estar; ser
be able to ser capaz de
be in charge of ser responsável por
beach praia
beautiful bonito(a)
because porque
become tornar-se
bed cama
bedroom quarto
before antes
begin começar
behave comportar-se
Behave yourself! Comporte-se!
behavior comportamento
behind atrás
believe acreditar
bell sino; sirene
belong pertencer
belongings pertences
below abaixo
besides além disso
best melhor
bet apostar
better melhor
between entre (duas pessoas ou objetos)
bicycle bicicleta
big grande
bike bicicleta
billion bilhão
biography biografia
birthday aniversário
bite morder
black preto(a)
blank lacuna
blending combinação, mistura
blind cego(a)
blue azul
body corpo
bomb bomba
bond elo, laço, vínculo
book livro
boot bota
bored entediado(a)
born nascer
borrow emprestar
boss chefe
both ambos
box caixa, quadro
boy garoto, menino
boyfriend namorado
brain cérebro
Brazilian brasileiro(a)
break quebrar
break the code decifrar o código
breakfast café da manhã
brief breve, curto(a)
bring trazer
bring up criar
British britânico(a)
brochure folheto
bronze bronze
brother irmão
brown marrom
brush escovar
build construir
building construção
built construído(a)
bus ônibus
business negócio
busy ocupado(a)
but mas
buy comprar
by de; por; por volta de

C

cake bolo
calculator calculadora
call chamar; telefonar; chamado; telefonema
calm calmaria
camp out acampar
can poder
cap boné
car carro
care preocupar-se
career carreira
carefully cuidadosamente
caring humanitário(a)
carry carregar
carry out realizar
case caso
cast elenco
castle castelo
casual casual
cat gato
category categoria
cause causa
caused causado(a)
cave caverna
CD player tocador de CD
celebrity celebridade
cell phone celular
central-west centro-oeste
century século
certain certo(a)
chain corrente
challenge desafio
chance chance
change mudar, trocar
charming encantador(a)
chart gráfico, quadro
chart topper artista no topo das paradas
cheap barato(a)
cheat trapacear
check assinalar; verificar
chess xadrez
chicken frango
child (pl. children) criança; filho(a)
chocolate chocolate
choose escolher

chop cortar, fatiar
Christmas Natal
chubby gorducho(a)
circular circular
city cidade
clap palma
class aula; classe
classical clássico(a)
classmate colega de classe
classroom sala de aula
clean limpar; limpo(a)
cleaner faxineiro(a)
cleanup limpeza
clear claro(a)
client cliente
climb subir em
clock relógio
clone clonar
close fechar
clothes roupas
club clube
C'mon! (Come on!) Vamos lá!
code código
coffee café
cognitive cognitivo(a)
cold frio(a); com frio; resfriado
college colégio
colonizer colonizador(a)
colony colônia
color cor
colored colorido(a)
column coluna
columnist colunista
combine combinar
come chegar, vir
come back voltar
Come on! Vamos lá!
come true tornar realidade
comfortable confortável
command comando
common comum
communication comunicação
community comunidade
companion companhia
company empresa
compare comparar
competition competição
complete completar; completo(a)
complicate complicar
composition produção textual; redação
compound composto(a)
comprehend compreender
computer computador
computer program programa de computador
computer programmer programador(a)
concentrate concentrar-se
concert concerto, *show*
condition condição; situação
confide confiar; contar segredo
Congratulations! Parabéns!
connect conectar
consequence consequência
consequently consequentemente
consider considerar
contain conter
content conteúdo
continuous contínuo(a)
continuously continuamente; sem parar
contribute contribuir
contributed doado(a)
control controlar
conversation conversa; conversação
convinced convicto(a)
cook cozinhar
Cool! Legal!
correct corrigir; correto(a)
correspond corresponder
corresponding correspondente
corruption corrupção
cost custar
count contar
country *country* (estilo musical); país
couple casal
courage coragem
cousin primo(a)
cover cobrir; capa
crane garça
crazy louco(a)
create criar
created criado(a)
creature criatura
critic crítico(a)
cross cruzar; riscar; cruz
cruise cruzeiro
cry chorar; gritar; apelo
cue dica
cultural cultural
culture cultura
cup copa (campeonato)
current atual
cut cortar
cute fofo(a)

D

dad papai
dance dançar; dança
dance moves passos de dança
dancer dançarino(a)
danger perigo
dangerous perigoso(a)
date data
daughter filha
day dia
dead morto(a), falecido(a)
deadly fatal
deaf surdo(a)
deal lidar
dear querido(a)
death morte
decade década
December dezembro
decide decidir
decision decisão
dedicated dedicado(a)
defensive defensivo(a)
definition definição
degree nível
delicious delicioso(a)
demand demanda
demonstrate demonstrar
dentist dentista
depend on depender de
describe descrever
description descrição
desert deserto
design desenhar; projetar
desperate desesperado(a)
dessert sobremesa
destination destino
detail detalhe

determination determinação
determine determinar
develop desenvolver
developed desenvolvido(a)
device dispositivo
dialogue diálogo
diary diário
dictatorship ditadura
dictionary dicionário
die morrer
diet dieta
difference diferença
different diferente
difficult difícil
dig cavar
digital digital
dinner jantar
diplomatic diplomático(a)
directed dirigido(a)
direction direção
directly diretamente
director diretor(a)
dirty sujo(a)
disappear desaparecer
disappointed decepcionado(a)
disapproval desaprovação
discarded descartado(a)
discover descobrir
disease doença
disguise disfarce
dishes louça
display dispor, exibir
distance distância
distant distante, longe
distraction distração
district bairro
diverse diverso(a)
diversity diversidade
dizziness tontura
do fazer
do the dishes lavar a louça
doctor médico(a)
document documento
dog cachorro
doll boneca
door porta
dormant dormente
doubt dúvida
down vertical (em uma palavra cruzada)
dragonfly libélula
drama drama
draw desenhar
drawing desenho
dream sonho
dress vestir; vestido
dried seco(a)
drink beber; bebida
drive dirigir
drop lançar
drum tamborilar; tambor; bateria
dry secar
dude cara (gíria)
due to devido a
during durante
Dutch holandês(esa)

E

each cada
each other um ao outro, uma à outra
eager ansioso(a)
ear ouvido
early cedo
Earth Terra (planeta)
easily facilmente
easy fácil
eat comer
edition edição
education educação
effectiveness eficiência
effect efeito; influência
egg ovo
elderly idoso(a)
elected eleito(a)
electric elétrico(a)
electronic eletrônico(a)
e-mail correio eletrônico, *e-mail*
emotional emocional
employ empregar
encourage encorajar; motivar
encouraged encorajado(a); motivado(a)
encyclopedia enciclopédia
end fim
end up acabar
energy energia
engineer engenheiro(a)
English Inglês (disciplina escolar)
enjoy gostar
entire inteiro(a), todo(a)
entry entrada
episode episódio; situação
escape escapar, fugir
especially em especial, especialmente
estimated estimado(a)
ethnically etnicamente
European europeu, europeia
even até mesmo; mesmo
event evento
ever alguma vez
every cada; todo(a), todos(as)
everybody todos; todo mundo
everyday todo dia
everything tudo
everywhere todos os lugares
evidence evidência
evident evidente, visível
exactly exatamente
exam prova, teste
example exemplo
except fora
exchange intercâmbio
excited empolgado(a)
exciting empolgante
exclusive exclusivo
exercise exercício
exhibit exibir; exposição
exist existir
exotic exótico(a)
expect esperar
expensive caro(a)
experience experiência
experiment experimento
expert especialista
explain explicar
explanation explicação
expose expor
express expressar
expression expressão
extra a mais
extracted from extraído(a) de
extremely extremamente
eye olho

F

fable fábula
face face, rosto
fact fato, realidade
factor fator
factory fábrica
fade into desaparecer
fall cair
false falso(a)
fame fama
family família
famous famoso(a)
fan fã
farm fazenda
fast rápido(a)
father pai
favor favor
favorite favorito(a)
feature característica
February fevereiro
feed alimentar
feel sentir
feeling sentimento
female fêmea; feminino(a)
festival festival
fever febre
few pouco(a), poucos(as)
field área; campo
fight luta
fighter lutador(a)
fill preencher
fill in completar; preencher
filled cheio(a)
film filmar; filme
final final
finance finança
find achar (acreditar); encontrar
fine ótimo(a)
Fine Arts belas-artes
finish acabar
finished acabado(a)
fire demitir, despedir
firefighter bombeiro(a)
firm firme
fishing rod vara de pescar
fix consertar
float flutuar
floor chão
flour farinha
fly voar
fly away voar
fold dobrar
folded dobrado(a)
folder panfleto
folk folclórico(a)
folklore folclore
follow seguir
following seguinte
food comida
foot (pl. feet) pé
for para, por
forced forçado(a)
forest floresta
forget esquecer
for instance por exemplo
form formar; forma
formal formal
former antiga, ex-
formidable formidável
free livre
freezing congelante
French francês(esa); Francês (disciplina escolar)
French fries batatas fritas
frequently frequentemente
fresh fruit fruta fresca
Friday sexta-feira
fridge geladeira
friend amigo(a)
friendship amizade
from de (origem)
fruit fruta
fuel combustível
full completo(a)
fun diversão
function função
future futuro(a); futuro
futurologist futurólogo(a)

G

gain ganhar; ganho
gallery galeria
game jogo
garage garagem
garbage lixo
garden jardim
gate portão
general geral
generation geração
generous generoso(a)
genius gênio
genre gênero
German alemão(ã)
get ficar; ganhar; obter; receber; ter
get away escapar; libertar-se
get into entrar
get some rest descansar um pouco
get up levantar
ghost fantasma
gift presente
giraffe girafa
girl garota, menina
girlfriend namorada
give dar
global global
glossary glossário
go ir
go across atravessar
go back voltar
go camping acampar
go on vacation sair de férias
go out acabar (luz); sair
go to bed ir dormir
goal objetivo
God Deus
god deus
gold ouro
goldfish peixe-dourado
gone acabado(a)
good bom, boa
good luck boa sorte
gossip fofoca
govern administrar, governar
government governo
grade nota
graffiti grafite (desenhos em muros e construções)
grammar gramática
grandpa vovô
grandchild (pl. grandchildren) neto
grandfather avô
grandma vovó
grandmother avó

grandparents avós
grant conceder
grape uva
graphical gráfico(a)
great grande
grid quadro
groom arrumar-se
group grupo
grow crescer
grow up crescer (tornar-se adulto)
guess adivinhar
guinea pig porquinho-da-índia
guitar violão
guy cara (gíria)
gym academia, ginásio

H

habit hábito
hair cabelo
hamburger hambúrguer
hamster hamster
hand mão
hand-operated operado manualmente
hang out passar um tempo com alguém
happen acontecer
happy alegre, feliz
hat chapéu
hate odiar
hatred ódio
have ter
have breakfast tomar café da manhã
have dinner jantar
have lunch almoçar
he ele
headache dor de cabeça
health saúde
healthy saudável
hear ouvir
heart coração
heavy pesado(a)
height altura
Hello! Olá!
helmet capacete
help ajudar; ajuda
her ela; dela
here aqui
hers dela
herself ela mesma
Hi! Oi!
hidden escondido(a)
high alto(a)
him ele
himself ele mesmo
his dele
history história
History História (disciplina escolar)
hobby *hobby*
hold apoiar; segurar
home casa, lar
homework lição de casa
honest honesto(a)
honesty honestidade
honey mel
hope esperança
horror horror
horse cavalo
hospital hospital
hospitalized hospitalizado(a)
hostile hostil
hot quente
hotel hotel
hour hora
house casa
housewife dona de casa
how como
How about…? E em relação a…?; Que tal…?
How long? Por quanto tempo?
How many? Quantos(as)?
How much? Quanto? Quanto custa?
How old? Quantos anos?
however entretanto
huge enorme
human humano(a)
human being ser humano
hung pendurado(a)
hungry faminto(a)
hurt machucar
husband marido

I

I eu
ice cream sorvete
idea ideia
if se
Illustrate ilustrar
image imagem
imagine imaginar
immediately imediatamente
immigrant imigrante
important importante
impressed impressionado(a)
impressive impressivo(a)
improve melhorar
in em, no, na
in need of com necessidade de
in order to a fim de
in parentheses entre parênteses
in return de volta
in the morning de manhã
in trouble em perigo; em encrenca
in turn em troca, em contrapartida
include incluir
incorporated incorporado(a)
incorrect incorreto(a)
increase aumentar
incredible incrível
indefinite indefinido(a)
Indian indiano(a)
individual individual
individuality individualidade
inferred deduzido(a)
infinitive infinitivo
influence influenciar; influência
information informação(ões)
initially inicialmente
initiative iniciativa
inscribed inscrito(a)
inside dentro, dentro de
inspire inspirar
instead em vez disso
institution instituição
instruction instrução
instrument instrumento
intelligence inteligência
intense intenso(a)
intensive intensivo(a)
interconnected interconectado(a)
interest interesse
interesting interessante
interface interface
international internacional

interrogative interrogativo(a)
interval intervalo
interview entrevista
into em; para dentro de
invasion invasão
invite convidar
involve envolver
involved envolvido(a)
issue assunto
it isso; ele(a) (usado para objetos e animais)
Italian italiano(a)
item item
its dele(a) (usado para objetos e animais)
itself ele mesmo, ela mesma (usado para objetos e animais)

J

jacket jaqueta
January janeiro
Japanese japonês(esa)
jazz *jazz*
jeans calça *jeans*
job trabalho, emprego
join associar; juntar-se
journal jornal
journey jornada
judgment juízo; julgamento
juice suco
junk food comida que não é saudável
just acabar de; apenas, somente

K

keep guardar, vigiar; manter
key chave
keyboard teclado
kid criança, garoto(a)
killed morto(a)
kilt saia escocesa
kind tipo
kind of meio, um pouco
kindly gentilmente
king rei
kingdom reino
kiss beijar
kitchen cozinha
kite pipa
kitten gatinho
know conhecer; saber

L

lady senhora
lake lago
lament lamentar
language idioma, língua
large grande
last último(a)
last up durar (tempo)
late depois
lately ultimamente
later mais tarde; tempos depois
later on depois disso
latex látex
launched lançado(a)
laundry roupas para lavar
law lei
leader líder
leaf folha
learn aprender
leave deixar, partir
left restante
left behind deixado(a) para trás
leg perna
legend lenda
lemon limão
less menos
lesson lição
let deixar, permitir
Let's... Vamos...
letter carta; letra
leukemia leucemia
level nível
librarian bibliotecário(a)
library biblioteca
lie mentira
life vida
light luz
like gostar; como; semelhante
list lista
listen ouvir
literature literatura
Lithuanian lituano(a)
little pequeno(a)
live morar; viver
lively cheio(a) de energia; vivaz
living room sala de estar
lock trancar
lonely sozinho(a)
long comprido(a); longo(a)
long ago há muito tempo
look olhar; parecer; aparência
look for buscar, procurar
look like aparentar, parecer
look up procurar
lose perder
lots of muitos(as)
loud alto(a) (volume)
loudspeaker caixa de som
love amar; amor
loyalty lealdade
lunch almoço
lyrics letra de música

M

machine máquina
made feito(a)
magazine revista
magic mágico(a)
mailbox caixa de correio
main principal
mainly principalmente
maintain conservar, manter
major maior
make fazer; tornar
mall *shopping center*
mambo mambo
man (pl. men) homem
manage administrar; dirigir
many muitos(as)
map mapa
marathon maratona
married casado(a)
martial-arts artes marciais
master mestre
match associar; ligar, unir
material material
Math Matemática (disciplina escolar)
mathematical matemático(a)
matter problema
maturity maturidade
may poder (verbo)
May maio
maybe talvez

me me; mim
meal refeição
mean significar
meaning significado
meaningful significativo(a)
mechanic mecânico(a)
mechanical mecânico(a)
medicine remédio
Medicine medicina
meet conhecer; encontrar
melodic melódico(a)
melody melodia
mention mencionar
mentioned mencionado(a)
menu cardápio
mess bagunça
message mensagem
metal metal
meter metro
mile milha
milk leite
Milky Way Via Láctea
million milhão
mind mente
mine meu(s), minha(s)
mines minas
minister ministro(a)
minute minuto
mirror espelho
miss sentir falta
missing ausente
mistake erro
mixture mistura
model modelo
modern moderno(a)
mom mamãe
moment momento
Monday segunda-feira
money dinheiro
monkey macaco
month mês
monument monumento
mood humor
moon lua
moonlight luar
more mais
morning manhã
most maioria; mais
mother mãe
motorbike motocicleta
mountain montanha
mourn lamentar; ficar de luto
mouse (pl. mice) rato
mouth boca
move mudar-se
moved comovido(a)
movement movimento
movie filme
movies cinema
Mr. sr. (senhor)
Mrs. sra. (senhora)
much muito
mom mãe
museum museu
music música
musical musical
musical instrument instrumento musical
musician musicista
must dever
my meu(s); minha(s)
myself eu mesmo(a)

N

name nome
nation nação
national nacional
native nativo(a)
nature natureza
navigation navegação
near perto; próximo(a)
nearly quase
necklace colar
need precisar; necessidade
negative negativo(a)
neighbor vizinho(a)
neighborhood vizinhança
neighboring vizinho(a)
nervous nervoso(a)
network rede
never nunca
new novo(a)
news notícia(s)
newspaper jornal
next próximo(a)
nice agradável; legal
night noite
no não
no matter independentemente; não importa
Nobel Prize Prêmio Nobel
nobody ninguém
nope não
north norte
northeast nordeste
nose nariz
not não
not even nem mesmo
nothing nada
now agora
nowadays hoje em dia
nowhere lugar nenhum
nowhere else nenhum outro lugar
nuclear nuclear
number número
numerous numeroso(a)
nurse enfermeiro(a)
nutritionist nutricionista

O

obese obeso(a)
object objeto
o'clock em ponto
October outubro
of de
of course lógico; claro
of the da, do
off desligar; desligado(a)
offer oferecer
offered oferecido(a)
office escritório
official oficial
officially oficialmente
often frequentemente
Oh, Gosh… Essa não…
old antigo(a), velho(a)
on em cima de; em, no, na
Once upon a time… Era uma vez…
online conectado(a)
only apenas, somente
open abrir
opened aberto(a)
opening abertura
operation operação

opinion opinião
opposite oposto(a)
opposition oposição
option opção
or ou
orange laranja
order ordenar; ordem
organization empresa; organização
organize organizar
organizer organizador
origin origem
original original; primeiro(a)
originally originalmente
orphan órfão(ã)
other outro(s), outra(s)
our nosso(s), nossa(s)
ours nosso(s), nossa(s)
ourselves nós mesmos(as)
out loud em voz alta
outline contorno
over acabado(a); mais de
over and over muitas vezes; repetidamente
overall completo(a)
own próprio(a)
owner proprietário(a)

P

page página
pain dor
paint pintar; tinta
painter pintor(a)
painting pintura
pair par
pants calças
paper papel
paralyzed paralisado(a)
parentheses parênteses
parents pais
park parque
part parte
participate participar
participle particípio
party festa
pass passar
past passado
pay pagar
peace paz
pedestal pedestal
pen caneta
pencil lápis
penguin pinguim
perfect perfeito(a)
perform realizar
period período
person (pl. people) pessoa
personal pessoal
pet animal de estimação
pharmaceutical industry indústria farmacêutica
pharmacist farmacêutico(a)
phone telefone
photo foto
phrase frase
physical físico(a)
Physics Física (ciência)
piano piano
pick up buscar
picture figura, foto; imagem
pie torta
piece pedaço; peça
pig porco
pilot piloto
pipe encanamento
place casa, lar; lugar
plan plano; planejar
plane avião
planet planeta
plant planta
plantation plantação
play brincar; jogar; tocar (instrumento musical); peça de teatro
player jogador(a)
please por favor
plumber encanador(a)
point ponto
police polícia
politic político(a)
political político(a)
politically politicamente
politician político(a)
poor pobre
popular popular
Portuguese Português (disciplina escolar)
position posição
possessions pertences
possessive possessivo(a)
possible possível
post afixar, colar; publicar (internet)
post a question fazer uma pergunta
postcard cartão-postal
potato batata
poverty pobreza
powerful poderoso(a)
practice praticar
prayer oração, prece
precious precioso(a)
predict prever
prefer preferir
prepare preparar
present presente
presentation apresentação
president presidente
pretty muito
prevent evitar; prevenir
primary primário(a)
prime superior
prince príncipe
printer impressora
print impressão
prize preço
probably provavelmente
problem problema
process processar; processo
producer produtor(a)
product produto
production produção
productive produtivo(a)
profession profissão
professional profissional
professionally profissionalmente
professor professor(a) de faculdade
program programa
programme programa
prohibit proibir
prohibition proibição
project projeto
pronoun pronome
proposal proposta
protest protestar
provide fornecer
puberty puberdade

publish publicar
puppy cachorrinho
purse bolsa
put pôr
put out publicar
put to sleep sacrificar um animal

Q

question pergunta, questão
quiz teste

R

rabbit coelho
race corrida
racket raquete
radiation radiação
rain chover; chuva
raise funds levantar fundos
reach alcançar
reaction reação
read ler
ready pronto(a)
real real
realistic realístico(a)
reality realidade
realize perceber
really realmente
reason razão
receive receber
recent recente
recently recentemente
record disco
recreational club clube de lazer
recycling reciclagem
red vermelho(a)
refer referir-se
reflexive reflexivo(a)
refrigerator geladeira
region região
regional regional
rejected rejeitado(a)
related relacionado(a)
relations relações
relationship relacionamento
relative relativo(a)
relatives familiares
religion religião
rely on confiar em
remember lembrar-se
repair consertar
replace substituir
reply responder
report relatar; relatório
reporter repórter
represent representar
representation representação
required obrigatório(a), pedido(a)
research pesquisa
researcher pesquisador(a)
respect respeitar; respeito
respected respeitado(a)
respond responder
responsibility responsabilidade
responsible responsável
responsibly responsavelmente
rest descanso
restaurant restaurante
restore recuperar
restroom banheiro, toalete
résumé currículo
retirement aposentadoria
retirement home asilo
reuse reutilização
review crítica; revisão
reward recompensa
rewrite reescrever
rhyme rimar; rima
rhyming que rima
rhythm ritmo
rice arroz
rich rico(a)
ride andar de/a
right correto(a)
right now agora mesmo
risk risco
ritualistic ritualista
rob roubar
robot robô
robot-maid robô-empregada
robotic robótica
rock music *rock*
roller rolo para pintura
romance romance
room quarto; sala
routine rotina
rude rude
rule governar
run correr
running corrida
runtime duração
Russian russo(a)

S

sad triste
safari safári
sail navegar
salad salada
sales clerk atendente de loja; vendedor(a)
salsa salsa
salt sal
same mesmo(a)
sand areia
sandwich sanduíche
Saturday sábado
say dizer
scared assustado
scary assustado(a)
scene cena; cenário
school escola
Science Ciências (disciplina escolar)
scientific científico(a)
scientist cientista
score marcar, pontuar; pontuação
screen tela
sea mar
search procurar; busca, procura
secret segredo
secretary secretário(a)
secretly em segredo, secretamente
see ver
see someone sair ou ter um relacionamento rápido com alguém
See you! Até logo!, Até mais tarde!
seek procurar
seem parecer
self-defense autodefesa
sell vender
send enviar
sentence sentença
series série
serious grave; sério(a)
service serviço
session seção

set conjunto; situado(a)
set off partir
set the table por a mesa
several muitos(as)
shared compartilhado(a)
she ela
shelf prateleira
shirt camisa
shocked chocado(a)
shoe sapato
shoot filmar; filmagem
shop loja
shopping list lista de compras
short curto(a), pequeno(a)
shortage falta
should dever
show exibir, mostrar
shy tímido(a)
sick doente
side lado
silent silencioso(a)
silver prata
similar parecido(a), similar
simple simples
simply simplesmente
since desde
sing cantar
singer cantor(a)
sister irmã
situation situação
size tamanho
skateboard *skate*
ski esqui
skill habilidade
skin pele
sky céu
slave escravo(a)
sleep dormir
sleeping bag saco de dormir
sleepy com sono; sonolento(a)
slight leve
slow diminuir; lento(a)
small pequeno(a)
smell cheirar
smile sorrir
so então; dessa maneira; tão
soccer futebol
social social
society sociedade
sofa sofá
soft calmo(a); leve
soldier soldado
solidarity solidariedade
some algum(ns), alguma(s)
somebody alguém
someone alguém
something algo, alguma coisa
sometimes às vezes
somewhere algum lugar
son filho
song canção
soon logo
sophisticated sofisticado(a)
sore throat dor de garganta
Sorry! Desculpe-me!
sound som
source fonte
south sul
southeast sudeste
southwest sudoeste
space espacial
Spain Espanha
Spanish Espanhol (disciplina escolar)
speak falar
speaker caixa de som; alto-falante
special especial
specialized especializado(a)
spectator espectador(a)
speech discurso
speed velocidade
spend gastar; passar (tempo)
spin girar, rodar
spirit espírito
sport esporte
sports club clube esportivo
square quadrado(a)
stairs escada
stand ficar
star estrela
start começar
state afirmar; estado
station estação
statue estátua
stay ficar
still ainda
stone pedra
stop parar
store loja
storm tempestade
story história
strange estranho(a)
strawberry morango
street rua
street art arte de rua
street artist artista de rua
stress estresse
stringed de corda (instrumento musical)
strong forte
structure estrutura
stuck preso(a)
student estudante, aluno(a)
study estudar; estudo
study hard estudar muito
stuff coisa
style estilo
subject assunto
successful bem-sucedido(a)
such tal, tais
such as como
sugar cane cana-de-açúcar
suggestion sugestão
suitable adequado(a)
sun sol
Sunday domingo
sunny ensolarado(a)
supermarket supermercado
support apoiar; apoio
sure certo(a)
Sure! Com certeza!
surprise surpresa
survive sobreviver
sweater suéter
sweet doce
swim nadar
swimmer nadador(a)
symptom sintoma
system sistema

T

table mesa
take extrair; fazer; levar; pegar
take a shower tomar banho de chuveiro
take care of cuidar de

take over dominar
take part participar
tale conto
talk conversar; falar
tambourine tamborim
task tarefa
taxi táxi
tea chá
teach ensinar
teacher professor(a)
team grupo, time
technology tecnologia
teen adolescente
teenager adolescente
television televisão
tell dizer
tennis tênis (esporte)
tense tempo verbal
terrible terrível
test teste, prova
text texto
than que
Thank you! Obrigado(a)!
that aquele(a); aquilo; que
the o(s), a(s)
theater teatro
their deles, delas
them eles, elas
themselves eles(as) mesmos(as)
then após, em seguida
therapy terapia
there ali, lá
these estes(as)
they eles, elas
thief (pl. thieves) ladrão
thin magro(a)
thing coisa
think achar, pensar
thinking opinião
thirsty com sede; sedento(a)
this este(a)
those aqueles(as)
though embora
thousand mil
through por meio de
Thursday quinta-feira
ticket ingresso
tic-tac-toe jogo da velha
time hora; tempo; vez
tired cansado(a)
title título
toast torrada
today hoje
toilet banheiro
tomato tomate
tomorrow amanhã
tone tom
tonight esta noite, hoje à noite
too muito; também
tooth (pl. teeth) dente
top topo
total total
touch tocar
tourist turístico(a)
tourist attraction atração turística
tournament torneio
towards em direção a; para
tower torre
town cidade
toy brinquedo
traditional tradicional
train trem
train station estação de trem
trait característica
transform transformar
translation tradução
travel viajar
treat tratar
tree árvore
trench trincheira
trial and error tentativa e erro
tribute tributo
trip viagem
trophy troféu
trouble problema
truck caminhão
true verdadeiro(a)
trust confiar
truth verdade
try tentar
T-shirt camiseta
Tuesday terça-feira
turn away virar na direção contrária a algo
turn down abaixar
turn towards virar na direção de algo
TV televisão
TV channel canal de TV
TV news anchor âncora de telejornal
twin gêmeo(a)
type tipo
typesetting composição tipográfica
typewriter máquina de escrever
typical típico(a)
typically tipicamente

U

umbrella guarda-chuva
uncle tio
under embaixo de; sob
undergo submeter-se
underline sublinhar
underneath embaixo
understand entender
understanding compreensão
unemployment desemprego
unfortunately infelizmente
unhappy infeliz
uniform uniforme
unique único(a)
unit unidade
United States Air Force Força Aérea dos Estados Unidos
university universidade
unknown desconhecido(a)
unscramble desembaralhar
unstable instável
until até
us nos
use usar; uso
used usado(a)
user usuário(a)
usually geralmente

V

vacation férias
valley vale
value valorizar; valor
variety variedade
vary variar
verb verbo
verse verso
very muito
vet veterinário(a)

vice-versa vice-versa
village vila
violin violino
virtual virtual
visible visível
visit visitar; visita
visitor visitante
voice voz
voluntarily voluntariamente
volunteer voluntário(a)

W

wait esperar
wake up acordar
walk andar; passear; passeio
wall muro; parede
wallet carteira
want querer
war guerra
was / were born nasceu / nasceram
wash lavar
wash the dishes lavar a louça
waste gastar; esgoto
watch assistir a
water água
wax cera
way caminho; maneira
we nós
weak fraco(a)
weapon arma
wear usar, vestir
weather clima
Wednesday quarta-feira
week semana
weekend fim de semana
welcome bem-vindo(a)
well bem
well-being bem-estar
western do Velho Oeste; ocidental
wet molhado
what o que, que, qual
What about you? E você?, E quanto a você?
What's the matter with…? Qual é o problema com…?
What's up? E aí?
What's your name? Qual é o seu nome?
wheel roda
when quando
where onde
which qual, quais; que
while enquanto
white branco(a)
who quem
whole todo
whose de quem
why por que, por quê
wife esposa
win ganhar
wind vento
wind chime sino dos ventos
window janela
wing asa
winner ganhador(a)
wish desejar; desejo
with com
without sem
witness testemunhar
woman (pl. women) mulher
word palavra
work trabalhar; trabalho
workbook caderno de exercícios
worker trabalhador(a)
world mundo
worldwide mundialmente
worry preocupar-se
worse pior
worst o(a) pior
Would you like…? Você gostaria de…?
write escrever
wrong errado(a)

Y

yacht iate
yard jarda; quintal
Yeah! Sim!
year ano
year old ano de idade
yellow amarelo(a)
yes sim
yesterday ontem
yet ainda
you você
young jovem
your seu(s), teu(s), sua(s), tua(s)
yours seu(s), teu(s), sua(s), tua(s)
yourself (pl. yourselves) você mesmo

Z

zone área
zoo zoológico

Irregular Verbs

Infinitive	Simple Past	Past Participle	Translation
be	was / were	been	estar, ser
become	became	become	tornar-se
begin	began	begun	começar
bet	bet	bet	apostar
bite	bit	bitten	morder
break	broke	broken	quebrar
bring	brought	brought	trazer
build	built	built	construir
buy	bought	bought	comprar
choose	chose	chosen	escolher
come	came	come	chegar, vir
cost	cost	cost	custar
dig	dug	dug	cavar
do	did	done	fazer
drink	drank	drunk	beber
drive	drove	driven	dirigir
eat	ate	eaten	comer
fall	fell	fallen	cair
feed	fed	fed	alimentar
feel	felt	felt	sentir
fly	flew	flown	voar
forget	forgot	forgot/forgotten	esquecer
get	got	got, gotten	ficar; ganhar; obter; receber
give	gave	given	dar
go	went	gone	ir
grow	grew	grown	crescer
have	had	had	beber; comer; ter
hold	held	held	apoiar; segurar
hurt	hurt	hurt	machucar
keep	kept	kept	guardar, vigiar

Infinitive	Simple Past	Past Participle	Translation
know	knew	known	conhecer; saber
leave	left	left	deixar; partir
let	let	let	deixar, permitir
lose	lost	lost	perder
make	made	made	fazer; tornar
mean	meant	meant	significar
meet	met	met	conhecer; encontrar
pay	paid	paid	pagar
put	put	put	pôr
read	read	read	ler
ride	rode	ridden	andar de/a
run	ran	run	correr
say	said	said	dizer
see	saw	seen	ver
seek	sought	sought	procurar
sell	sold	sold	vender
send	sent	sent	enviar
shoot	shot	shot	filmar
show	showed	shown	exibir, mostrar
sing	sang	sung	cantar
sleep	slept	slept	dormir
spend	spent	spent	gastar; passar (tempo)
spin	span/spun	spun	girar, rodar
take	took	taken	extrair; fazer; levar; pegar
teach	taught	taught	ensinar
tell	told	told	dizer
undergo	underwent	undergone	submeter-se
understand	understood	understood	entender
wake up	woke up	woken up	acordar
wear	wore	worn	usar, vestir
win	won	won	ganhar
write	wrote	written	escrever

Track List

Track	Page	Unit	Exercise
1	Introduction		
2	8	1	2
3	12	1	11
4	15	1	Key Language
5	18	2	2
6	23	2	12
7	25	2	Key Language
8	28	3	2
9	32	3	10
10	35	3	Key Language
11	37	3	4
12	38	4	2
13	42	4	10
14	45	4	Key Language
15	47	4	4
16	48	5	2
17	53	5	13
18	55	5	Key Language
19	58	6	2
20	62	6	11
21	62	6	12
22	65	6	Key Language
23	68	7	2
24	73	7	10
25	75	7	Key Language
26	78	8	2
27	83	8	12
28	85	8	Key Language
29	87	8	3